YOUR COMPLETE TAURUS 2025 PERSONAL HOROSCOPE

Monthly Astrological Prediction Forecast Readings of Every Zodiac Astrology Sun Star Signs- Love, Romance, Money, Finances, Career, Health, Travel, Spirituality.

Iris Quinn

Alpha Zuriel Publishing

Your Complete Taurus 2025 Personal Horoscope/ Iris Quinn. - - 1st ed.

"Astrology is a language. If you understand this language, the sky speaks to you."

— IRIS QUINN

CONTENTS

CHAPTER ONE

TAURUS PROFILE

General Characteristics

- **Element:** Earth
- **Quality:** Fixed
- **Ruler:** Venus
- **Symbol:** The Bull
- **Dates:** April 20 - May 20

Personality Traits

- **Dependable:** Reliable and consistent in actions and commitments.
- **Patient:** Exhibits a calm and steady demeanor, willing to wait for the right moment.
- **Practical:** Focused on realistic and achievable goals, values tangible results.
- **Loyal:** Deeply faithful and dedicated to loved ones and friends.
- **Sensual:** Enjoys and appreciates physical pleasures and comfort.
- **Determined:** Possesses a strong willpower, not easily deterred from goals.

- **Stubborn:** Can be inflexible and resistant to change.
- **Hardworking:** Diligent and persistent in efforts.
- **Stable:** Provides a sense of security and reliability in relationships and endeavors.
- **Possessive:** Tends to hold on tightly to people and things.

Strengths

- **Reliability:** Can be counted on to follow through on promises and commitments.
- **Patience:** Able to wait for the right opportunity and sees projects through to the end.
- **Practicality:** Focuses on what is achievable and beneficial in the long term.
- **Loyalty:** Stays true to loved ones and stands by them in times of need.
- **Persistence:** Unyielding in the pursuit of goals, rarely gives up.
- **Sensuality:** Deeply appreciates beauty, luxury, and the finer things in life.

Weaknesses

- **Stubbornness:** Can be inflexible and resistant to new ideas or changes.
- **Possessiveness:** May struggle with letting go and can be overly attached.
- **Materialism:** Sometimes places too much value on possessions and wealth.

- **Rigidity:** Can be set in their ways, making it difficult to adapt to new situations.
- **Indulgence:** Tends to overindulge in physical pleasures and comforts.

Planets and Their Influences

- **Career Planet:** Saturn – Brings structure and a methodical approach to professional life.
- **Love Planet:** Venus – Governs affection, beauty, and romantic relationships.
- **Money Planet:** Venus – Also influences financial matters and a love for luxury.
- **Planet of Fun, Entertainment, Creativity, and Speculations:** Jupiter – Encourages enjoyment and expansion in creative pursuits.
- **Planet of Health and Work:** Mercury – Influences routine, health, and day-to-day activities.
- **Planet of Home and Family Life:** Moon – Rules emotions, instincts, and domestic affairs.
- **Planet of Spirituality:** Neptune – Represents dreams, intuition, and spiritual pursuits.
- **Planet of Travel, Education, Religion, and Philosophy:** Jupiter – Governs growth, learning, and philosophical outlooks.

Compatibility

- **Signs of Greatest Overall Compatibility:** Virgo, Capricorn
- **Signs of Greatest Overall Incompatibility:** Leo, Aquarius

- **Sign Most Supportive for Career Advancement:** Capricorn
- **Sign Most Supportive for Emotional Well-being:** Cancer
- **Sign Most Supportive Financially:** Virgo
- **Sign Best for Marriage and/or Partnerships:** Scorpio
- **Sign Most Supportive for Creative Projects:** Pisces
- **Best Sign to Have Fun With:** Sagittarius
- **Signs Most Supportive in Spiritual Matters:** Pisces
- **Best Day of the Week:** Friday

Additional Details

- **Colors:** Green, Pink
- **Gem:** Emerald
- **Scent:** Rose, Sandalwood
- **Birthstone:** Emerald
- **Quality:** Fixed (resolute and steady)

-

PERSONALITY OF TAURUS

Taurus, born between April 20 and May 20, is an earth sign governed by Venus, the planet of love and beauty. This connection to Venus gives Taurus individuals a deep appreciation for the finer things in life, such as comfort, luxury, and aesthetics. They find joy in the simple pleasures, like a well-cooked meal, a beautiful piece of art, or a cozy, inviting space.

People born under the Taurus sign are known for their dependability and reliability. They are the ones you can always count on to keep their promises and commitments. Their patience is one of their most remarkable traits. Taurus individuals are willing to wait for the right moment and do not rush into things. This calm and steady demeanor makes them excellent friends and partners, providing a sense of security and stability in relationships.

In matters of the heart, Taurus is incredibly loyal. Once they commit to someone, their dedication and steadfastness are unwavering. They go to great lengths to support and stand by their loved ones, making their loyalty a cornerstone of their personality. This makes them deeply valued by those who are close to them.

Practicality is another hallmark of Taurus. They focus on realistic and achievable goals, valuing tangible results over abstract ideas. This pragmatic approach helps them effectively navigate life's challenges, as they are always grounded and clear on what needs to be done.

Taurus individuals have a strong appreciation for the physical world. They are sensual beings who enjoy indulging in their senses, whether through good food, comfortable surroundings, or physical affection. Their love for nature and their eye for beauty in all forms often shine through in their personal spaces and lifestyles.

However, the determination and strong will of Taurus can sometimes manifest as stubbornness. They can be inflexible and resistant to change, preferring to stick with what they know works. This trait can lead to difficulties when faced with new situations or the need to adapt quickly.

Possessiveness is another aspect of the Taurus personality. They tend to hold tightly to their loved ones and possessions, which can sometimes create tension. It's important for them to find a balance between caring deeply and allowing space for growth and change.

Despite these challenges, Taurus individuals are undeniably hardworking. They are diligent and persistent, often putting in the necessary effort to achieve their goals. This persistence, combined with their practical mindset, helps them succeed in various aspects of life.

Taurus people are known for their stability and consistency. They provide a grounding presence in the lives of those around them, making them cherished companions. Their love for beauty, combined with their practical and loyal nature, creates a personality that is both nurturing and strong. With their feet firmly planted on the ground, Taurus individuals navigate life with a steady and determined approach, bringing a sense of security and joy to those around them.

WEAKNESSES OF TAURUS

Taurus, while known for their many admirable qualities, also has certain weaknesses that can pose challenges in their personal and professional lives. One of the most prominent traits of Taurus is their stubbornness. They have a strong will and once they set their mind on something, it's very difficult to change their course. This inflexibility can sometimes make it hard for them to adapt to new situations or consider other viewpoints, leading to potential conflicts with others who may see things differently.

Another notable weakness of Taurus is their tendency to be possessive. This trait can extend to both their relationships and their material possessions. In their relationships, they might hold on too tightly to their loved ones, which can lead to feelings of suffocation for their partner. Their need to control or protect what they deem important can sometimes come across as overbearing or clingy.

Taurus individuals also have a strong desire for comfort and security, which, while beneficial in many ways, can lead to a resistance to change. They prefer stability and predictability, and sudden changes or disruptions can cause significant stress and anxiety for them. This aversion to change can hinder their ability to take risks or embrace new opportunities that could lead to personal growth and development.

Materialism is another challenge for Taurus. Their appreciation for the finer things in life can sometimes turn into an excessive focus on acquiring material possessions. They might place too much value on wealth and luxury, which can lead to a superficial approach to life. This focus on material goods can sometimes distract them from more meaningful pursuits and relationships.

Additionally, Taurus can sometimes be perceived as overly self-reliant and reserved. They have a tendency to internalize their feelings and not share their burdens with others, which can lead to a buildup of stress and emotional fatigue. Their reluctance to ask for help or express vulnerability can create a barrier in their relationships, making it difficult for others to understand and support them fully.

Despite their generally calm and patient demeanor, Taurus can also experience bouts of jealousy and possessiveness. They can become insecure in their relationships if they feel threatened or uncertain about their partner's loyalty. This jealousy can lead to misunderstandings and conflicts, potentially damaging the trust and harmony in their relationships.

While Taurus' desire for stability and routine is often seen as a strength, it can also contribute to a reluctance to step out of their comfort zone. They might miss out on exciting opportunities and experiences because they prefer to stick with what they know. Their conservative approach to life can sometimes make them seem unadventurous or risk-averse to those around them.

In summary, while Taurus is known for their reliability, loyalty, and practicality, they must also navigate their tendency towards stubbornness, possessiveness, resistance to change, materialism, self-reliance, jealousy, and reluctance to step out of their comfort zone. By being aware of these weaknesses, Taurus individuals can work towards achieving a more balanced and fulfilling life, embracing flexibility and openness to new experiences while maintaining their inherent strengths.

RELATIONSHIP COMPATIBILITY WITH TAURUS

Based only on their Sun signs, this is how Taurus interacts with others. These are the compatibility interpretations for all 12 potential Taurus combinations. This is a limited and insufficient method of determining compatibility.

However, Sun-sign compatibility remains the foundation for overall harmony in a relationship.

The general rule is that yin and yang do not get along. Yin complements yin, and yang complements yang. While yin and yang partnerships can be successful, they require more effort. Earth and water zodiac signs are both Yin. Yang is represented by the fire and air zodiac signs.

Taurus with Yin Signs (Earth and Water)

Taurus and Taurus (Yin with Yin):

When two Taurus individuals come together, the relationship is marked by stability, reliability, and a deep mutual understanding. Both partners share similar values and goals, enjoying a life filled with comfort and consistency. Their relationship thrives on mutual respect and a shared love for the finer things in life. However, their stubbornness can lead to clashes if neither is willing to compromise. Patience and open communication are key to maintaining harmony and ensuring that both partners feel valued and heard.

Taurus and Virgo (Yin with Yin):

Taurus and Virgo create a highly compatible and harmonious partnership. Both signs are practical, detail-oriented, and value stability. Virgo's meticulous nature complements Taurus' steadiness, making them an effective team in both personal and professional aspects of life. They appreciate each other's reliability and work ethic, building a relationship based on mutual respect and shared goals. Their only challenge lies in Virgo's tendency to be overly critical, which Taurus may find frustrating. Communication and understanding can help them navigate these moments and strengthen their bond.

Taurus and Capricorn (Yin with Yin):

This pairing is characterized by mutual ambition, practicality, and a strong work ethic. Taurus and Capricorn both value stability and long-term success, making them a powerful and determined duo. Capricorn's discipline and strategic approach to life complement Taurus' persistence and practicality. They support each other's goals and create a stable, secure environment. Their biggest challenge might be their reluctance to express emotions, which can lead to misunderstandings. Open communication and emotional vulnerability are essential to deepen their connection.

Taurus and Cancer (Yin with Yin):

Taurus and Cancer form a nurturing and emotionally fulfilling relationship. Both signs value security, home, and family, creating a loving and supportive environment. Taurus provides the stability and consistency that Cancer craves, while Cancer offers the emotional depth and nurturing that Taurus appreciates. Their shared love for comfort and home life strengthens their bond. However, Taurus' stubbornness and Cancer's sensitivity can sometimes clash. Patience and empathy are crucial to resolving conflicts and maintaining harmony.

Taurus and Scorpio (Yin with Yin):

Taurus and Scorpio have a deeply intense and magnetic connection. These opposite signs are drawn to each other's strengths, creating a powerful and transformative relationship. Taurus is attracted to Scorpio's depth and passion, while Scorpio admires Taurus' stability and reliability. Their relationship is marked by strong loyalty and commitment. However, both signs can be possessive and stubborn, leading to power struggles. Learning to compromise and communicate openly can help them harness their strengths and build a lasting bond.

Taurus and Pisces (Yin with Yin):

Taurus and Pisces create a gentle and harmonious partnership. Taurus' practicality and stability provide a grounding influence for Pisces' dreamy and emotional nature. Pisces brings creativity and empathy to the relationship, helping Taurus explore new perspectives. They share a deep emotional connection and a mutual appreciation for beauty and comfort. However, Taurus' need for stability can clash with Pisces' tendency to be indecisive. Patience and understanding are essential for balancing their

differences and fostering a supportive and loving
relationship.

Taurus with Yang Signs (Fire and Air)

Taurus and Aries (Yin with Yang):

Taurus and Aries have contrasting energies that
can make their relationship both challenging and
exciting. Taurus values stability and routine, while
Aries is dynamic and seeks constant adventure. Aries
can introduce excitement and spontaneity into Taurus'
life, encouraging them to step out of their comfort
zone. Conversely, Taurus can offer Aries the
grounding and patience they need. For this
relationship to work, both partners need to appreciate
their differences and find a balance between stability
and adventure. Open communication and mutual
respect are key to making this partnership thrive.

Taurus and Gemini (Yin with Yang):

Taurus and Gemini have very different approaches
to life, which can create both challenges and
opportunities for growth. Taurus is steady and values

routine, while Gemini is curious, adaptable, and seeks variety. Taurus may find Gemini's unpredictability unsettling, while Gemini might see Taurus as too rigid. However, if they can appreciate each other's strengths, they can learn a lot from one another. Taurus can benefit from Gemini's flexibility and open-mindedness, while Gemini can gain stability and consistency from Taurus. Patience, compromise, and clear communication are essential to making this relationship work.

Taurus and Leo (Yin with Yang):

Taurus and Leo have a relationship characterized by warmth, loyalty, and a mutual appreciation for the good things in life. Both signs enjoy luxury and comfort, which can create a harmonious connection. However, their strong personalities can sometimes clash. Leo's need for attention and admiration may conflict with Taurus' desire for a more low-key and stable lifestyle. Taurus might see Leo as too demanding, while Leo may find Taurus too stubborn. To make this relationship work, both partners need to practice compromise and understand each other's needs for validation and stability.

Taurus and Libra (Yin with Yang):

Taurus and Libra, both ruled by Venus, share a love for beauty, harmony, and the finer things in life. This common ground can create a deep and aesthetically pleasing connection. However, their approaches to life can differ. Taurus is practical and grounded, while Libra is more social and seeks balance in relationships. Taurus may find Libra's indecisiveness frustrating, while Libra might see Taurus as too rigid. Communication and mutual respect are crucial for balancing their differences and creating a harmonious partnership.

Taurus and Sagittarius (Yin with Yang):

Taurus and Sagittarius have very different energies, which can make their relationship challenging but potentially rewarding. Taurus values stability and routine, while Sagittarius is adventurous and seeks constant change. Sagittarius can bring excitement and new experiences into Taurus' life, encouraging them to be more spontaneous. Conversely, Taurus can offer Sagittarius a sense of grounding and security. For this relationship to work, both partners need to appreciate their differences and find a balance between stability and adventure.

Patience, understanding, and a willingness to compromise are key to making this partnership successful.

Taurus and Aquarius (Yin with Yang):

Taurus and Aquarius have contrasting natures that can create both challenges and opportunities for growth. Taurus is practical, stable, and values routine, while Aquarius is innovative, independent, and seeks change. Taurus may find Aquarius' unpredictability unsettling, while Aquarius might see Taurus as too conservative. However, if they can appreciate each other's strengths, they can learn a lot from one another. Taurus can benefit from Aquarius' open-mindedness and progressive thinking, while Aquarius can gain stability and consistency from Taurus. Patience, compromise, and clear communication are essential to making this relationship work.

In conclusion, Taurus' compatibility with other sun signs varies widely based on the yin and yang theory. Earth and water signs generally complement Taurus' stable and nurturing nature, leading to harmonious and fulfilling relationships. Fire and air signs, while presenting more challenges, can provide excitement

and growth, requiring more effort to navigate their
differences. With mutual respect, understanding, and
a willingness to learn from each other, Taurus can
form successful and balanced partnerships with any
sign.

LOVE AND PASSION

Taurus, ruled by Venus, the planet of love and beauty, embodies a deeply passionate and romantic nature. Their approach to love is steadfast and unwavering, reflecting their need for security, stability, and deep emotional connections. Taurus individuals are sensual beings who appreciate the physical and emotional aspects of a relationship, valuing both touch and tenderness.

When a Taurus falls in love, they do so wholeheartedly and with great intensity. They are not ones to rush into relationships impulsively; instead, they take their time to truly get to know their partner and ensure that the connection is genuine and solid. This careful approach stems from their desire for long-term stability and their aversion to fleeting or superficial connections. Once committed, a Taurus is fiercely loyal and devoted, viewing their partner as a cornerstone of their life.

Passion for a Taurus is expressed through consistent and thoughtful actions rather than grandiose gestures. They are the type of partner who will remember small details about their loved one, showing their affection through meaningful gifts, comforting touches, and by creating a warm and inviting home environment. Physical touch is crucial for Taurus; they communicate their love through hugs, kisses, and intimate moments, making their partner feel cherished and secure.

In love, Taurus seeks a deep emotional connection. They crave a partner who can match their level of commitment and who is willing to invest in building a strong, enduring bond. This earth sign values honesty and straightforward communication, expecting their partner to be open and sincere. Taurus individuals are not interested in games or drama; they desire a relationship built on mutual respect, trust, and a shared vision for the future.

Romantic at heart, Taurus finds immense joy in creating special moments and experiences for their loved ones. They enjoy planning romantic dinners, surprise getaways, and cozy nights in, all designed to foster closeness and intimacy. Their love for beauty and comfort often translates into a desire to surround their partner with luxury and warmth, making them feel pampered and appreciated.

However, the intense loyalty and possessiveness of a Taurus can sometimes be challenging. They may struggle with feelings of jealousy or insecurity if they perceive any threat to the relationship. It's important for their partner to reassure them of their love and commitment regularly, helping to alleviate these fears. In turn, Taurus must work on trusting their partner and giving them the space to maintain their individuality.

Taurus individuals are also known for their stubbornness, which can lead to conflicts if not managed properly. They are firm in their beliefs and can be resistant to change, preferring to stick to what they know and trust. For a relationship with a Taurus to thrive, both partners need to practice patience and understanding, finding ways to compromise and respect each other's viewpoints.

Despite these potential challenges, the love and passion of a Taurus are unmatched. They bring a sense of stability, warmth, and unwavering dedication to their relationships, making their partner feel truly valued and secure. Their blend of sensuality, practicality, and emotional depth creates a rich and fulfilling romantic experience. A Taurus in love is a partner who will stand by you through thick and thin, always ready to offer their love, support, and affection in abundance.

MARRIAGE

Marriage for Taurus is a sacred commitment, reflecting their deep desire for stability, security, and long-term companionship. Known for their loyalty and dependability, Taurus individuals approach marriage with seriousness and dedication. They seek to build a strong foundation with their partner, valuing consistency and mutual respect above all else. To keep a Taurus happy in marriage, it's crucial to understand their need for a harmonious and comfortable home life. Creating an environment that is both physically and emotionally nurturing is key. Taurus thrives on routine and predictability, so maintaining a steady and calm atmosphere helps them feel secure. Regularly expressing affection and appreciation reinforces their sense of being valued, which is essential for their happiness.

Taurus men in marriage are deeply devoted and protective. They take their role as a husband seriously, striving to provide and care for their family. A Taurus man appreciates a partner who recognizes and respects his efforts. He values practical expressions of love, such as cooking a meal, managing household responsibilities, or supporting his goals. Stability and loyalty are paramount for a Taurus man, and he is

drawn to partners who are equally committed and
reliable. To make a marriage work with a Taurus man,
it's important to be patient and understanding of his
need for consistency. Encouraging open
communication and creating a space where he feels
comfortable expressing his feelings can strengthen the
bond. Being attentive to his need for physical affection,
such as hugs, kisses, and cuddling, helps keep the
romance alive and makes him feel cherished.

Taurus women in marriage bring warmth, love, and
a nurturing spirit. They are often the glue that holds the
family together, ensuring that everyone feels cared for
and supported. A Taurus woman values a partner who
appreciates her efforts and reciprocates her loyalty. She
seeks a harmonious and beautiful home, where she can
express her love through creating a comfortable and
inviting environment. A Taurus woman is deeply
romantic and enjoys small gestures of love and
appreciation from her partner. To maintain a happy
marriage with a Taurus woman, it's essential to be
reliable and consistent. She values a partner who can
share in the responsibilities of maintaining a stable and
comfortable life. Demonstrating affection regularly,
both through words and actions, reassures her of your
love and commitment. Celebrating special occasions
and creating lasting memories together enhances the
emotional connection.

The secret to making a marriage with a Taurus work lies in understanding and respecting their core values of stability, loyalty, and comfort. Taurus individuals dislike sudden changes or disruptions, so keeping a steady and predictable routine helps them feel secure. Being honest and straightforward in communication fosters trust and prevents misunderstandings. It's important to be patient with their stubbornness, recognizing that their resistance to change often stems from a desire to protect what they cherish.

In a marriage, Taurus appreciates a partner who shares their appreciation for the finer things in life. They enjoy indulging in good food, beautiful surroundings, and moments of relaxation. Planning regular date nights, celebrating anniversaries, and spending quality time together helps keep the relationship vibrant and fulfilling. Encouraging Taurus to pursue their interests and hobbies also contributes to their happiness and sense of fulfillment.

A key aspect of keeping Taurus happy in marriage is maintaining physical intimacy. They are sensual beings who crave touch and affection. Regular physical contact, whether it's holding hands, hugging, or intimate moments, strengthens the bond and reassures them of your love. Being attentive to their emotional

needs and providing reassurance during times of
insecurity helps maintain harmony.

In conclusion, marriage with a Taurus is a journey
of deep commitment, stability, and mutual respect. By
understanding their need for consistency, creating a
nurturing environment, and expressing love through
both words and actions, you can build a strong and
lasting partnership. Taurus individuals bring a sense of
warmth and security to their marriages, making them
dedicated and loving partners who value the enduring
bond of matrimony.

CHAPTER TWO

TAURUS 2025 HOROSCOPE

Overview Taurus 2025

(April 20 - May 20)

2025 is poised to be a year of significant change, growth, and self-discovery for those born under the steadfast sign of Taurus. As the planets traverse the celestial landscape, they will bring a dynamic mix of challenges and opportunities that will shape your journey throughout the year, encouraging you to embrace transformation while staying grounded in your values and sense of security.

The year commences with a powerful planetary concentration in the Fire signs, igniting your passion for exploration and personal development. Jupiter, the planet of expansion and growth, spends the first half of the year in your 3rd House of communication, short trips, learning, and skills. This is a fantastic time to broaden your horizons through education, workshops, or online courses. Engage in stimulating conversations with siblings, neighbors, or colleagues, and remain open to fresh ideas and perspectives. Your curiosity and desire for knowledge will be at an all-time high, so embrace this opportunity to enhance your skills and expand your mindset.

However, on June 9, Jupiter shifts gears and enters Cancer, your 4th House of home, family, and emotional foundations. This transition brings a more nurturing and protective energy to your domestic life and inner world. You may feel a strong urge to create a comfortable and secure living space, spend quality time with loved ones, and explore your emotional roots. This is an excellent time to focus on home improvement projects, family bonding, and strengthening your sense of belonging.

As Jupiter moves through Cancer, it will form challenging square aspects to Saturn in Aries (June 15) and Neptune in Aries (June 18), both in your 12th

House of spirituality, solitude, and endings. These transits may bring up deep-seated fears, doubts, or limiting beliefs that need to be confronted and released. You may experience a period of introspection and soul-searching as you grapple with questions of faith, purpose, and surrender. Lean into your Taurean strength and practicality to find grounding during these times of uncertainty. Remember that growth often involves letting go of what no longer serves you to make space for new beginnings.

The Lunar Nodes, powerful points of destiny and growth, will spend the year moving through Aries and Libra, activating your 12th and 6th Houses. The North Node in Libra invites you to cultivate more balance, harmony, and cooperation in your daily routines and work life. Focus on creating a healthy work-life balance, nurturing supportive relationships with colleagues, and finding joy in service to others. The South Node in Aries may challenge you to release the need for constant self-reliance and control, learning to trust in the flow of life and accept help when needed.

Eclipses will play a pivotal role in your journey this year, particularly those occurring in Taurus and Scorpio, your 1st and 7th Houses of self and partnerships. Lunar eclipses in Scorpio on May 13 and November 7 may bring significant shifts or endings in your closest relationships, both personal and professional. Use these intense energies to dive deep into your emotional depths, exploring issues of intimacy, power, and shared resources. Be willing to confront any shadows or imbalances in your partnerships, working towards greater authenticity and transformation.

Solar eclipses in Taurus on October 21 and April 29 will shine a powerful spotlight on your sense of self, personal identity, and unique path forward. These cosmic wildcards may bring unexpected opportunities for growth, change, and new beginnings. Embrace the chance to reinvent yourself, make bold moves, and step into your power. Trust your inner compass and let your values guide you through any upheavals or uncertainties.

A major astrological event occurs on March 23 when Saturn, the planet of structure, responsibility, and maturity, enters Aries, your 12th House of spirituality and inner work. This transit, lasting until 2026, marks the beginning of a profound journey of self-reflection, healing, and letting go. Saturn will challenge you to confront your deepest fears, doubts, and limiting patterns, inviting you to do the hard work of self-mastery and spiritual growth. While this transit may feel isolating or challenging at times, it is a powerful opportunity to build a solid foundation of inner strength, resilience, and self-awareness. Embrace solitude, meditation, and therapeutic practices to navigate this transformative period.

Another significant shift takes place on March 23 when Pluto, the planet of power, transformation, and rebirth, moves into Aquarius, your 10th House of career and public image. This transit, lasting until 2044, will bring a profound restructuring of your professional life and long-term goals. You may feel called to step into a leadership role, make bold career moves, or align your work with your deepest passions and values. Pluto will challenge you to confront any power dynamics or hidden agendas in your professional life, inviting you to claim your authority and make a meaningful impact in the world. Trust the process of destruction and regeneration, knowing that what falls away is making space for a more authentic and empowered version of yourself to emerge.

Your ruling planet Venus will have an eventful year, starting with an extended visit to Aries, your 12th House of spirituality and transcendence. From July 22 to September 3, Venus will be retrograde in this sensitive sector, inviting you to dive deep into your inner world and explore your hidden desires, fears, and creative potential. This is a profound time for healing, forgiveness, and letting go of the past. You may feel a strong urge to retreat, reflect, and connect with your intuition. Trust the messages and insights that arise during this period, as they will guide you towards greater self-love, compassion, and spiritual growth.

On June 21, a powerful Venus-Mars conjunction at the last degree of Aries will bring a potent opportunity for release, transformation, and new beginnings. This cosmic reset button will help you break free from old patterns, wounds, and limitations, paving the way for a more authentic and empowered expression of yourself. Embrace the energy of courage, passion, and self-assertion, and trust that you have the strength to move forward with clarity and purpose.

After this intense period of inner work, Venus will grace your sign from September 3 to October 8, bringing a much-needed dose of self-love, beauty, and pleasure. This is a wonderful time to focus on self-care, pampering, and expressing your unique style and creativity. You may also experience a surge of romantic interest or opportunities for financial abundance. Embrace the energy of self-worth, value, and deserving, knowing that you are worthy of love, respect, and success.

In the second half of the year, the astrological focus shifts to the nurturing and intuitive Water signs. Jupiter's entry into Cancer on May 18 will bring a renewed sense of emotional connection, security, and belonging. This is a wonderful time to deepen your bonds with family, explore your ancestral roots, and create a nurturing home environment. You may also feel a strong urge to explore your creativity, intuition, and emotional intelligence. Trust your instincts and let your heart guide you towards experiences and relationships that feel nourishing and supportive.

Mars, the planet of action, energy, and desire, will tour nostalgic Cancer from August 23 to October 15, activating your 4th House of home, family, and emotional foundations. This transit may bring up old memories, patterns, or family dynamics that need to be addressed and healed. You may feel more sensitive, moody, or protective during this time, so be sure to prioritize self-care and set healthy boundaries with loved ones. Channel any excess energy into home improvement projects, cooking, or nurturing your inner child.

As Mars moves into Scorpio, your 7th House of partnerships, from October 15 to January 9, 2025, you can expect a surge of passion, intensity, and transformation in your closest relationships. This is a

powerful time to confront any issues of power, control,
or intimacy in your partnerships, working towards
greater depth, honesty, and mutual empowerment. You
may also feel a strong urge to collaborate with others
on shared goals or projects, pooling your resources and
talents for maximum impact. Just be mindful of
potential conflicts or power struggles, and strive to find
a balance between asserting your needs and
considering the needs of others.

On the financial front, 2025 looks to be a promising
year for Taureans, with Jupiter bringing opportunities
for growth, expansion, and abundance. If you are self-
employed or in a creative field, the first half of the year
is particularly favorable for marketing your skills,
attracting new clients, or launching innovative
projects. Your natural Taurean gifts of practicality,
perseverance, and financial savvy will serve you well,
especially in the latter part of the year when many
planets cluster in grounded Earth signs. Focus on
creating a solid budget, saving for the future, and
investing in your long-term security and stability.

As the year comes to a close, you can look back on
2025 as a year of profound growth, transformation, and
self-discovery. While change and uncertainty may
have felt uncomfortable at times for your stability-
loving sign, trust that the challenges you've faced have

served to strengthen your resilience, adaptability, and inner power. You've learned to embrace change as an opportunity for growth, to trust your instincts and values, and to let go of what no longer serves you. As you move forward into 2026 and beyond, know that you have the inner resources, wisdom, and courage to create a life that is truly authentic, meaningful, and fulfilling. Keep shining your unique light, Taurus, and trust that the universe is guiding you towards your highest good. Here's to a year of growth, abundance, and joyful self-discovery!

January 2025

Overview Horoscope for the Month:

Welcome to January 2025, Taurus! This month marks the beginning of a transformative year filled with opportunities for personal growth, emotional healing, and spiritual awakening. With a powerful stellium of planets in Capricorn activating your 9th house of higher learning, travel, and philosophy, you are being called to expand your horizons, challenge your beliefs, and seek new adventures that broaden your perspective on life.

The New Moon in Aquarius on January 29th falls in your 10th house of career and public image, bringing fresh energy and innovative ideas to your professional life. This is a time to step outside your comfort zone, embrace your unique talents and skills, and make bold moves towards your long-term goals and aspirations.

Love:

In love, January 2025 is a month of deep emotional connection and spiritual intimacy. With Venus, your ruling planet, entering dreamy Pisces on January 2nd, you may find yourself craving a soul-level bond with your partner or seeking a relationship that transcends the physical realm. This is a time to open your heart, express your feelings with vulnerability and authenticity, and create a safe space for love to flourish.

If you're in a committed relationship, take time to connect with your partner through shared spiritual practices, such as meditation, yoga, or dream work. Explore the deeper meaning and purpose of your union, and find ways to support each other's personal and spiritual growth.

If you're single, you may find yourself attracted to people who share your values, beliefs, and spiritual path. Look for partners who inspire you to be your best self, who challenge you to grow and evolve, and who offer emotional depth and understanding. Trust your intuition and let your heart guide you towards meaningful connections.

Career:

In your career, January 2025 is a month of ambition,
achievement, and public recognition. With a powerful
stellium of planets in Capricorn activating your 10th
house of career and public image, you are being called
to step into your power, claim your authority, and make
your mark in the world. This is a time to set clear goals,
create a strategic plan, and take practical steps towards
your long-term vision of success.

The New Moon in Aquarius on January 29th brings
fresh energy and innovative ideas to your professional
life. Trust your unique talents and skills, and don't be
afraid to think outside the box and try new approaches.
Network with like-minded individuals who share your
vision and values, and seek out mentors who can guide
you towards your highest potential.

If you're considering a career change or starting a
new business, do your research and make sure that your
plans are grounded in reality. Focus on building a
strong foundation of skills, experience, and
relationships that can support you in the long run.

Finances:

In finances, January 2025 is a month of practicality, responsibility, and long-term planning. With Saturn, the planet of structure and discipline, traveling through your 8th house of shared resources and investments, you are being called to take a serious look at your financial situation and make wise choices that support your long-term security and stability.

Review your budget, identify areas where you can save and invest, and make sure that your financial decisions align with your values and goals. If you have any debts or financial obligations, create a realistic plan to pay them off and free yourself from unnecessary burdens.

Consider seeking the advice of a financial planner or advisor who can help you navigate any challenges and make the most of your resources. Trust your own judgment and instincts, and don't be afraid to make necessary changes or adjustments to your financial strategy.

Health:

In health, January 2025 is a month of vitality, resilience, and inner strength. With Mars, the planet of energy and action, entering nurturing Cancer on January 6th, you may find yourself feeling more introspective and focused on your emotional well-being. This is a time to listen to your body's needs and rhythms, and to prioritize activities that bring you a sense of comfort, security, and inner peace.

Take time to engage in gentle exercise, such as yoga, walking, or swimming, that helps you feel grounded and centered. Nourish your body with healthy, whole foods that support your immune system and energy levels. Make sure to get plenty of rest and sleep, and create a bedtime routine that helps you unwind and release any stress or tension from the day.

On an emotional level, practice self-compassion and kindness towards yourself. Acknowledge any feelings of anxiety, fear, or uncertainty that may arise, and offer yourself the same love and support that you would offer a dear friend. Seek out activities that bring you joy, creativity, and a sense of connection to something greater than yourself.

Travel:

In travel, January 2025 may bring opportunities for long-distance journeys or spiritual pilgrimages that expand your mind, heart, and soul. With a powerful stellium of planets in Capricorn activating your 9th house of travel, higher learning, and philosophy, you are being called to step outside your comfort zone and explore new horizons that broaden your perspective on life.

Consider booking a trip to a place that holds deep spiritual significance for you, such as a sacred site, a retreat center, or a natural wonder that inspires awe and reverence. Seek out experiences that challenge your beliefs, open your mind to new ideas and cultures, and deepen your connection to the greater mysteries of life.

If travel isn't possible or practical, find ways to bring a sense of adventure and exploration into your daily life. Enroll in a course or workshop that expands your knowledge and skills, read books or watch documentaries that introduce you to new concepts and perspectives, or engage in spiritual practices that help you connect with a higher power or purpose.

Insights from the Stars:

The celestial energies of January 2025 remind you
of the power of faith, surrender, and spiritual growth.
With Venus in Pisces activating your 11th house of
hopes, wishes, and community, you are being called to
connect with like-minded souls who share your vision
of a better world and support you on your path of
personal and collective evolution.

The New Moon in Aquarius on January 29th invites
you to embrace your unique talents and skills, to think
outside the box and innovate in your career and public
life, and to trust in the power of your own creativity
and vision. Let go of any limiting beliefs or fears that
may be holding you back, and have faith in your ability
to manifest your dreams and goals.

Remember that you are a powerful creator and co-
creator, and that your thoughts, emotions, and actions
have the power to shape your reality and contribute to
the greater good. Stay open to the guidance and support
of the universe, and trust that everything is unfolding
in perfect timing and alignment with your highest
purpose and potential.

Best Days of the Month:

January 2nd: Venus enters Pisces, bringing a dreamy, romantic, and imaginative energy to your friendships, social life, and community involvement.

January 6th: Mars enters Cancer, activating your 3rd house of communication, learning, and short trips. This is a great time to express your feelings, learn new skills, and explore your local environment.

January 11th: The True Node enters Pisces, highlighting your spiritual growth, soul's evolution, and connection to a higher purpose or calling.

January 29th: The New Moon in Aquarius invites you to embrace your unique talents and skills, innovate in your career and public life, and connect with like-minded individuals who share your vision and values.

January 30th: Uranus turns direct in Taurus, bringing sudden insights, breakthroughs, and positive changes to your sense of self, identity, and personal freedom. Trust your instincts and let your authentic self shine.

February 2025

Overview Horoscope for the Month:

Welcome to February 2025, Taurus! This month promises to be a time of deep emotional healing, spiritual growth, and positive change. With the Sun traveling through your 10th house of career and public image for most of the month, you are being called to step into your power, claim your authority, and make your mark in the world. Trust in your unique talents and abilities, and don't be afraid to take bold steps towards your long-term goals and aspirations.

The Full Moon in Leo on February 12th illuminates your 4th house of home, family, and emotional foundations. This is a time to nurture your closest relationships, create a safe and comfortable living space, and connect with your roots and inner sense of security. Let go of any past wounds or patterns that may be holding you back, and embrace the healing power of love, forgiveness, and self-acceptance.

Love:

In love, February 2025 is a month of passion, creativity, and self-expression. With Venus, your ruling planet, entering fiery Aries on February 4th, you may find yourself feeling more bold, assertive, and confident in your romantic pursuits. This is a time to take the lead in your relationships, express your desires with clarity and conviction, and attract partners who appreciate your unique qualities and strengths.

If you're in a committed relationship, take time to reignite the spark of passion and adventure with your partner. Plan a special date or getaway that allows you to break free from your usual routines and explore new experiences together. Be open and honest about your needs and desires, and work together to create a dynamic of mutual respect, support, and growth.

If you're single, you may find yourself attracted to people who are confident, independent, and unafraid to take risks. Look for partners who inspire you to be your best self, who challenge you to step outside your comfort zone, and who appreciate your unique talents and abilities. Trust your instincts and let your heart guide you towards meaningful connections.

Career:

In your career, February 2025 is a month of recognition, achievement, and positive change. With the Sun illuminating your 10th house of career and public image, you are being called to step into the spotlight and showcase your unique talents and abilities. This is a time to take on new challenges, pursue your long-term goals with passion and determination, and make your mark in your chosen field.

The Full Moon in Leo on February 12th brings a sense of completion and culmination to your professional endeavors. Trust in the work you've put in, and be open to receiving recognition and rewards for your efforts. If you've been considering a career change or starting a new business, this is a powerful time to take action and manifest your vision into reality.

Seek out mentors, colleagues, and collaborators who share your values and support your growth. Network with like-minded individuals who can offer guidance, resources, and opportunities for advancement. Stay focused on your long-term goals, and don't be afraid to take calculated risks that align with your authentic self and purpose.

Finances:

In finances, February 2025 is a month of abundance, prosperity, and positive change. With Jupiter, the planet of expansion and abundance, traveling through your 2nd house of money and resources, you are being called to embrace a mindset of abundance and trust in the flow of the universe. This is a time to release any fears or limiting beliefs around scarcity or lack, and to open yourself up to new opportunities for income and wealth.

Review your budget, identify areas where you can save and invest, and make sure that your financial decisions align with your values and long-term goals. Consider seeking the advice of a financial planner or advisor who can help you create a strategy for growth and stability. Trust your own judgment and instincts, and be open to unexpected sources of income or support.

On a deeper level, reflect on your relationship with money and abundance. What beliefs or patterns may be holding you back from experiencing true prosperity and fulfillment? How can you cultivate a sense of gratitude, generosity, and trust in the universe? Remember that you are a powerful creator and co-creator, and that your thoughts and actions have the power to shape your financial reality.

Health:

In health, February 2025 is a month of vitality, resilience, and inner growth. With Mars, the planet of energy and action, traveling through your 3rd house of communication and learning, you may find yourself feeling more curious, expressive, and mentally active. This is a time to feed your mind with new ideas and perspectives, engage in stimulating conversations and debates, and explore new ways of thinking and communicating.

Take time to engage in activities that challenge your mind and keep you mentally sharp, such as reading, writing, or learning a new skill. Be open to different viewpoints and opinions, and practice active listening and empathy in your interactions with others. At the same time, be mindful of your words and the impact they can have on others. Speak from a place of kindness, compassion, and understanding.

On a physical level, make sure to get plenty of rest and exercise to support your immune system and overall well-being. Consider incorporating more plant-based foods into your diet, and limit your intake of processed or inflammatory foods. Take breaks throughout the day to stretch, breathe deeply, and connect with your body's natural rhythms and needs.

Travel:

In travel, February 2025 may bring opportunities for short trips or adventures that feed your mind and soul. With Mars activating your 3rd house of communication and learning, you may find yourself drawn to destinations that offer intellectual stimulation, cultural enrichment, or new experiences. Consider booking a trip to a museum, art gallery, or historical site that piques your curiosity and expands your knowledge.

If travel isn't possible or practical, find ways to bring a sense of adventure and exploration into your daily life. Take a different route to work, try a new restaurant or cuisine, or attend a local event or workshop that introduces you to new ideas and perspectives. Be open to serendipity and spontaneity, and trust that the universe will bring you the experiences and connections you need for your growth and evolution.

Insights from the Stars:

The celestial energies of February 2025 remind you of the power of authenticity, self-expression, and positive change. With Venus in Aries activating your 12th house of spirituality and inner growth, you are being called to connect with your deepest desires, fears, and dreams. This is a time to release any masks or facades you may be wearing, and to embrace your true self with courage and vulnerability.

The Full Moon in Leo on February 12th illuminates your 4th house of home, family, and emotional foundations. Trust in the healing power of love, forgiveness, and self-acceptance, and let go of any past wounds or patterns that may be holding you back. Surround yourself with people who support and inspire you, and create a living space that reflects your authentic self and values.

Remember that you are a powerful creator and co-creator, and that your thoughts, emotions, and actions have the power to shape your reality and contribute to the greater good. Stay open to the guidance and support of the universe, and trust that everything is unfolding in perfect timing and alignment with your highest purpose and potential.

Best Days of the Month:

February 4th: Venus enters Aries, bringing a bold, passionate, and confident energy to your spiritual growth and inner transformation.

February 5th: The First Quarter Moon in Taurus invites you to take practical steps towards your long-term goals and aspirations, and to trust in your own judgment and instincts.

February 12th: The Full Moon in Leo illuminates your home, family, and emotional foundations, bringing a sense of completion and culmination to your personal life and relationships.

February 16th: Pallas enters Aquarius, activating your 10th house of career and public image. This is a great time to bring innovative ideas and strategic thinking to your professional pursuits.

February 27th: The New Moon in Pisces invites you to connect with your intuition, imagination, and spiritual purpose. Set intentions for healing, growth, and positive change in all areas of your life.

March 2025

Overview Horoscope for the Month:

Welcome to March 2025, Taurus! This month promises to be a time of profound transformation, spiritual awakening, and new beginnings. The astrological energies align to support your journey inward, encouraging you to confront your fears, release limiting patterns, and connect with your soul's true purpose. Embrace the opportunities for self-discovery and trust in the wisdom of the universe as you navigate this powerful time.

March 2025 is a significant month for you, Taurus, as Saturn enters your 12th house of spirituality and inner growth on the 1st. This transit, lasting until 2026, marks the beginning of a profound journey of self-reflection, healing, and letting go. You are called to do the deep inner work of confronting your fears, releasing old patterns and beliefs, and connecting with your soul's true calling. Embrace solitude, introspection, and self-reflection, trusting in the guidance of the universe.

The New Moon in Aries on March 29th falls in your
12th house, amplifying the themes of spiritual
awakening and emotional release. Set intentions for
healing, forgiveness, and inner peace, knowing that the
universe supports you in your growth and
transformation.

Love:

In love, March 2025 emphasizes the importance of
emotional depth, vulnerability, and spiritual intimacy.
With Venus, your ruling planet, in sensitive Pisces for
most of the month, you may crave a soul-level
connection with your partner or seek a relationship that
transcends the superficial. Open your heart, express
your feelings authentically, and create a safe space for
love to flourish.

For committed Taureans, focus on strengthening
your bond through shared spiritual practices, deep
conversations, and acts of compassion. Single
Taureans may find themselves attracted to individuals
who share their values, offer emotional understanding,
and inspire personal growth. Trust your intuition and
let your heart guide you toward meaningful
connections.

Career:

Your career sector is influenced by Saturn's transit through your 12th house, prompting a period of introspection, reflection, and inner growth. You may question your current path or seek a deeper sense of purpose and meaning in your professional life. Reassess your goals, values, and priorities, ensuring that your work aligns with your authentic self and soul's calling.

Trust that the universe is guiding you toward your highest potential, even if the path is not always clear. Seek guidance from mentors or spiritual advisors who can support you in your journey of self-discovery and transformation.

Finances:

In finances, March 2025 is a month of spiritual abundance, trust, and surrender. With Venus and Jupiter activating your 12th house, you are called to release fears or limiting beliefs around money and embrace a mindset of gratitude and faith. Trust in the flow and provision of the universe, knowing that you will always be supported.

Review your budget, identify areas where you can
give back or share your resources, and ensure that your
financial decisions align with your spiritual values.
Consider setting aside a portion of your income for
charitable donations or tithing, trusting that the more
you give, the more you will receive.

Health:

Your physical and emotional well-being are
highlighted this month, as the cosmic energies support
your journey of spiritual healing, self-care, and inner
peace. With the Sun in Pisces illuminating your 12th
house, honor your body's natural rhythms and prioritize
activities that bring you calm, relaxation, and renewal.

Engage in gentle, restorative practices like yoga,
meditation, or aromatherapy, and surround yourself
with soothing environments. Nourish your body with
whole, natural foods, and limit exposure to stress and
negativity. Practice self-compassion, forgiveness, and
acceptance, allowing yourself to process emotions in
healthy ways.

Travel:

March 2025 may bring opportunities for spiritual retreats, pilgrimages, or journeys of self-discovery. With Saturn in your 12th house, you may feel called to visit sacred sites, connect with nature, or explore new spiritual practices and traditions. Consider planning a trip to a destination that holds deep meaning and significance for you.

If travel is not possible, find ways to bring a sense of adventure and exploration into your daily life. Take walks in nature, visit local spiritual centers, or attend workshops that introduce you to new ideas and perspectives. Remain open to synchronicity and divine guidance, trusting in the experiences and connections that arise.

Insights from the Stars:

The celestial energies of March 2025 remind you of the power of surrender, faith, and inner wisdom. Saturn's entry into your 12th house calls you to let go of control, trust in the greater plan of the universe, and connect with your deepest truth and purpose. Embrace the unknown, face your fears and shadows, and allow yourself to be transformed by the power of divine love and grace.

The New Moon in Aries on March 29th brings a powerful opportunity for healing, forgiveness, and new beginnings in your spiritual life. Set intentions for inner peace, emotional release, and positive change, knowing that the universe supports you every step of the way. Remember that you are a divine being of light and love, and your soul's purpose is to shine your unique gifts in service to the world.

Best Days of the Month:

March 1st: Saturn enters Aries, activating your 12th house of spirituality and inner growth. A powerful time for self-reflection, introspection, and inner transformation begins.

March 6th: The First Quarter Moon in Gemini invites you to communicate your feelings and ideas authentically, seeking new perspectives that support your growth.

March 14th: The Full Moon in Virgo brings a powerful opportunity for healing, self-care, and service. Trust your intuition and find ways to share your gifts with the world.

March 20th: The Sun enters Aries, marking the beginning of the astrological new year and a cycle of growth and transformation. Set intentions for the year ahead, trusting in the power of new beginnings.

March 29th: The New Moon in Aries falls in your 12th house, bringing a potent time for healing, forgiveness, and spiritual awakening. Set intentions for inner peace, emotional release, and positive change, trusting in the universe's guidance and support.

April 2025

Overview Horoscope for the Month:

Welcome to April 2025, Taurus! This month promises to be a time of powerful transformation, new beginnings, and personal growth. With the Sun traveling through your 12th house of spirituality and inner work for most of the month, you are being called to connect with your deepest self, release old patterns and beliefs, and embrace a new level of self-awareness and inner wisdom. This is a time to trust in the power of surrender, faith, and divine timing, and to allow yourself to be guided by your intuition and higher purpose.

The New Moon Solar Eclipse in Taurus on April 29th falls in your 1st house of self and identity, bringing a powerful opportunity for personal transformation, self-discovery, and new beginnings. Set intentions for the next six months and beyond, and trust that the universe is supporting you in creating a life that aligns with your authentic self and soul's purpose.

Love:

In matters of the heart, April 2025 emphasizes the importance of emotional intimacy, vulnerability, and spiritual connection. With Venus, your ruling planet, in sensitive Pisces until the 12th, you may find yourself craving a deep, soulful bond with your partner or seeking a relationship that transcends the superficial. Open your heart, express your feelings with authenticity, and create a safe space for love to blossom.

As Venus moves into fiery Aries on the 30th, you may experience a shift towards a more passionate, assertive, and independent approach to love. Embrace this energy to express your desires, set clear boundaries, and attract relationships that honor your individuality and strength.

Career:

In your career, April 2025 is a month of inner growth, self-reflection, and spiritual alignment. With the Sun traveling through your 12th house of spirituality and inner work, you may find yourself questioning your current path or seeking a deeper sense of purpose and meaning in your professional life. This is a time to reassess your goals, values, and priorities, and to make sure that your work aligns with your authentic self and soul's calling.

Take time to reflect on your strengths, weaknesses, and areas for growth, and be willing to let go of any limiting beliefs or patterns that may be holding you back. Seek out mentors, coaches, or spiritual guides who can support you in your journey of self-discovery and transformation. Trust that the universe is guiding you towards your highest potential and purpose, even if the path is not always clear or easy.

If you're considering a career change or starting a new business, the New Moon Solar Eclipse in Taurus on April 29th is a powerful time to set intentions and take action towards your dreams. Trust in your unique talents and abilities, and don't be afraid to take risks or step outside your comfort zone. Remember that your work is a reflection of your soul's purpose, and that you have the power to create a life and career that brings you joy, fulfillment, and abundance.

Finances:

In finances, April 2025 is a month of spiritual abundance, trust, and surrender. With Venus traveling through your 12th house of spirituality and inner growth for the first part of the month, you are being called to release any fears or limiting beliefs around money and abundance, and to trust in the flow and provision of the universe. This is a time to cultivate a mindset of gratitude, generosity, and faith, and to open yourself up to unexpected sources of income and support.

Review your budget, identify areas where you can give back or share your resources with others, and make sure that your financial decisions align with your spiritual values and beliefs. Consider setting aside a portion of your income for charitable donations, tithing, or other forms of giving that bring you joy and fulfillment. Trust that the more you give, the more you will receive, and that the universe will always provide for your needs and desires.

On a deeper level, reflect on your relationship with money and abundance, and any past wounds or traumas that may be blocking your flow of wealth and prosperity. Practice forgiveness, release, and self-love, and affirm your worthiness and deserving of all good things. Remember that true abundance comes from within, and that your inner state of being is the foundation for your external reality.

Health:

Your physical and emotional well-being are highlighted this month, as the cosmic energies support your journey of healing, release, and inner peace. With the Sun and Mercury in your 12th house, prioritize activities that promote relaxation, introspection, and spiritual connection, such as meditation, yoga, or energy healing.

Pay attention to any physical symptoms or emotional discomfort that may arise, as they may be messages from your body and soul guiding you towards greater self-care and balance. Practice self-compassion, forgiveness, and acceptance, and seek support from trusted healers or therapists if needed.

Travel:

In travel, April 2025 may bring opportunities for spiritual retreats, pilgrimages, or journeys of self-discovery. With the Sun traveling through your 12th house of spirituality and inner work, you may feel called to visit sacred sites, connect with nature, or explore new spiritual practices and traditions. Consider booking a trip to a place that holds deep meaning and significance for you, such as a monastery, ashram, or natural wonder.

If travel isn't possible or practical, find ways to bring a sense of adventure and exploration into your daily life. Take a nature walk, visit a local temple or church, or attend a spiritual workshop or event that introduces you to new ideas and perspectives. Be open to synchronicity and divine guidance, and trust that the universe will bring you the experiences and connections you need for your growth and evolution.

Insights from the Stars:

The celestial energies of April 2025 remind you of the power of surrender, faith, and inner wisdom. With the Sun traveling through your 12th house of spirituality and inner work, you are being called to let go of control, trust in the greater plan of the universe, and connect with your deepest truth and purpose. This is a time to embrace the unknown, face your fears and shadows, and allow yourself to be transformed by the power of divine love and grace.

The New Moon Solar Eclipse in Taurus on April
29th brings a powerful opportunity for personal
transformation, self-discovery, and new beginnings.
Set intentions for the next six months and beyond, and
trust that the universe is supporting you in creating a
life that aligns with your authentic self and soul's
purpose. Remember that you are a divine being of light
and love, and that your journey is unfolding in perfect
timing and alignment with your highest good.

Best Days of the Month:

April 4th: Saturn sextile Uranus, bringing a
harmonious blend of structure and innovation, tradition
and progress. This is a great time to make positive
changes in your life that align with your long-term
goals and aspirations.

April 7th: Mercury goes direct in Pisces, bringing
clarity and forward momentum to your
communication, ideas, and plans. Trust your intuition
and inner guidance, and express yourself with
authenticity and compassion.

April 12th: The Full Moon in Libra illuminates your
6th house of health, work, and service, bringing a sense

of balance and harmony to your daily routines and relationships. Focus on self-care, collaboration, and finding joy in the present moment.

April 21st: Saturn conjunct the True Node, bringing a powerful opportunity for spiritual growth, karmic healing, and alignment with your soul's purpose. Trust in the wisdom of the universe, and let go of any obstacles or limitations that are holding you back.

April 29th: The New Moon Solar Eclipse in Taurus falls in your 1st house of self and identity, bringing a powerful opportunity for personal transformation, self-discovery, and new beginnings. Set intentions for the next six months and beyond, and trust in the power of your own strength, beauty, and worth.

May 2025

Overview Horoscope for the Month:

Taurus, May 2025 is a month of profound change, growth, and new beginnings for you. The astrological energies are intense and transformative, with a series of powerful planetary alignments and eclipses shaking up the status quo and calling you to step into your power and purpose. This is a time to let go of the past, embrace the present, and trust in the unfolding of your future.

The month begins with the Sun in your sign, illuminating your 1st house of self and identity. This is your time to shine, Taurus, and to celebrate your unique gifts, talents, and qualities. You may feel a renewed sense of confidence, vitality, and purpose, and a desire to express yourself more fully and authentically in the world.

However, the Full Moon Lunar Eclipse in Scorpio on May 13th will bring intense emotions and revelations to the surface, particularly in your 7th house of partnerships and relationships. This eclipse will challenge you to confront any fears, secrets, or power dynamics that may be holding you back from true intimacy and connection. It's time to let go of any toxic patterns or relationships that no longer serve your highest good, and to open yourself up to deeper levels of trust, vulnerability, and transformation.

Love:

In love, May 2025 is a month of passion, intensity, and transformation. With Venus, your ruling planet, traveling through fiery Aries for most of the month, you may feel a renewed sense of desire, confidence, and assertiveness in your romantic life. This is a time to take the lead in your relationships, express your needs and desires openly and honestly, and attract partners who appreciate your strength and independence.

If you're in a committed relationship, the Full Moon Lunar Eclipse in Scorpio on May 13th will bring any underlying issues or power struggles to the surface. This is an opportunity to have deep, honest conversations with your partner about your fears, desires, and boundaries, and to work together to create

a more authentic and intimate connection. Be willing
to let go of any expectations or attachments that may
be holding you back from true love and vulnerability.

If you're single, this eclipse may bring unexpected
encounters or revelations that challenge your beliefs
about love and relationships. Stay open to new
possibilities and perspectives, and trust that the
universe is guiding you towards the right person at the
right time. Focus on healing any past wounds or
traumas, and cultivating a deep sense of self-love and
self-worth.

Career:

In your career, May 2025 is a month of ambition,
innovation, and breakthrough. With Mars, the planet of
action and energy, traveling through your 10th house
of career and public image for most of the month, you
may feel a renewed sense of drive, determination, and
leadership in your professional life. This is a time to
take bold steps towards your goals and dreams, and to
assert your unique talents and abilities in the world.

However, the Full Moon Lunar Eclipse in Scorpio
on May 13th may bring unexpected changes or
challenges to your career path or public reputation.

This eclipse will expose any hidden agendas, power struggles, or fears that may be holding you back from true success and fulfillment. It's time to let go of any limiting beliefs or patterns, and to trust in your own inner guidance and intuition.

Stay open to new opportunities and collaborations that align with your values and purpose, and be willing to take calculated risks and think outside the box. You may need to confront any fears or doubts that arise, and to trust in your own resilience and adaptability. Remember that your career is a reflection of your soul's journey, and that every challenge is an opportunity for growth and transformation.

Finances:

In finances, May 2025 is a month of abundance, prosperity, and breakthrough. With Venus traveling through your 2nd house of money and resources for the first part of the month, you may experience unexpected windfalls, opportunities, or insights that help you to manifest your financial goals and dreams. This is a time to trust in the flow and abundance of the universe, and to cultivate a mindset of gratitude, generosity, and positive expectation.

However, the Full Moon Lunar Eclipse in Scorpio on May 13th may bring any hidden fears, blocks, or power struggles around money and resources to the surface. This eclipse will challenge you to confront any limiting beliefs or patterns that may be holding you back from true financial freedom and empowerment. It's time to let go of any scarcity mentality or attachment to material possessions, and to focus on creating a sense of inner wealth and fulfillment.

Review your budget, investments, and financial plans, and make any necessary adjustments or changes that align with your values and goals. Consider seeking the guidance of a trusted financial advisor or mentor who can help you to navigate any challenges or opportunities that arise. Remember that your relationship with money is a reflection of your relationship with yourself, and that true abundance comes from within.

Health:

In health, May 2025 is a month of vitality, resilience, and transformation. With the Sun traveling through your sign for most of the month, you may feel a renewed sense of energy, strength, and well-being. This is a time to prioritize your physical, mental, and emotional health, and to cultivate daily practices and habits that support your overall vitality and resilience.

However, the Full Moon Lunar Eclipse in Scorpio on May 13th may bring any hidden fears, traumas, or blocks around your health and well-being to the surface. This eclipse will challenge you to confront any self-sabotaging behaviors or patterns that may be holding you back from true healing and transformation. It's time to let go of any unhealthy attachments or addictions, and to focus on creating a sense of inner peace and balance.

Take time to rest, recharge, and listen to your body's needs and signals. Engage in activities that bring you joy, relaxation, and a sense of connection to your inner self, such as meditation, yoga, or spending time in nature. Nourish your body with healthy, whole foods, and limit your exposure to toxins, stress, and negative influences.

Travel:

In travel, May 2025 may bring unexpected opportunities for adventure, exploration, and personal growth. With Mars traveling through your 9th house of travel, higher education, and philosophy for most of the month, you may feel a strong desire to expand your horizons, learn new things, and experience different cultures and perspectives.

Consider taking a trip or enrolling in a course or workshop that aligns with your interests and passions. This is a time to step outside your comfort zone, challenge your assumptions and beliefs, and open yourself up to new ideas and possibilities.

However, the Full Moon Lunar Eclipse in Scorpio on May 13th may bring any hidden fears, anxieties, or power struggles around travel and exploration to the surface. This eclipse will challenge you to confront any limiting beliefs or patterns that may be holding you back from true freedom and adventure. It's time to let go of any attachments to safety or security, and to trust in the journey of your soul.

Insights from the Stars:

The celestial energies of May 2025 remind you of the power of transformation, authenticity, and self-mastery. With the Sun illuminating your sign, and the Full Moon Lunar Eclipse in Scorpio activating your 7th house of partnerships and relationships, you are being called to step into your full power and potential, and to let go of any masks, illusions, or limitations that no longer serve your highest good.

This is a time to embrace your shadow, face your fears, and trust in the wisdom and guidance of the universe. You are a powerful creator and manifester, and your thoughts, beliefs, and actions have the power to shape your reality and attract your deepest desires and dreams.

Stay open to the unexpected, and trust that every challenge or setback is an opportunity for growth, learning, and transformation. Remember that you are a divine being of love and light, and that your soul's journey is unfolding in perfect timing and alignment with your highest good.

Best Days of the Month:

May 1st: Uranus sextile the True Node, bringing unexpected insights, breakthroughs, and opportunities for growth and change. Trust your intuition and be open to new possibilities and perspectives.

May 4th: The First Quarter Moon in Leo invites you to take bold steps towards your goals and dreams, and to express your unique creativity and passion in the world.

May 13th: The Full Moon Lunar Eclipse in Scorpio brings intense emotions and transformative energies to your relationships and partnerships. Let go of any toxic patterns or attachments, and open yourself up to deeper levels of intimacy, vulnerability, and connection.

May 18th: Jupiter sextile Chiron and square the True Node, bringing opportunities for healing, growth, and alignment with your soul's purpose. Trust in the wisdom of your wounds, and let go of any limiting beliefs or patterns that no longer serve you.

May 25th: The New Moon in Gemini invites you to set intentions around communication, learning, and self-expression. Trust in the power of your voice and your ideas, and be open to new perspectives and possibilities.

June 2025

Overview Horoscope for the Month:

Taurus, June 2025 is a month of emotional depth, spiritual growth, and personal empowerment for you. The astrological energies are intense and transformative, with a series of powerful planetary alignments and eclipses inviting you to dive deep into your inner world, confront your shadows, and emerge with a renewed sense of purpose and passion.

The month begins with Venus, your ruling planet, entering your sign on June 6th, bringing a heightened sense of beauty, sensuality, and self-worth to your life. This is a time to celebrate your unique qualities and talents, and to attract abundance, love, and joy into your world. However, Venus will also form a challenging square aspect to Saturn in Pisces on June 12th, asking you to confront any fears, doubts, or limitations that may be holding you back from true intimacy and connection.

The New Moon in Gemini on June 25th will activate your 2nd house of money, resources, and self-worth, inviting you to set powerful intentions around abundance, prosperity, and financial freedom. This is a time to trust in your own value and worth, and to cultivate a mindset of gratitude, generosity, and positive expectation.

Love:

In love, June 2025 is a month of emotional intensity, spiritual growth, and deep connection. With Venus traveling through your sign for most of the month, you may feel a heightened sense of magnetism, charm, and desirability. This is a time to express your love and affection openly and authentically, and to attract partners who appreciate your unique qualities and talents.

If you're in a committed relationship, the Venus-Saturn square on June 12th may bring any underlying fears, doubts, or limitations to the surface. This is an opportunity to have honest, vulnerable conversations with your partner about your needs, desires, and boundaries, and to work together to create a more authentic and intimate connection. Be willing to let go of any expectations or attachments that may be holding you back from true love and vulnerability.

If you're single, the New Moon in Gemini on June 25th may bring unexpected opportunities for love and romance. Stay open to new possibilities and perspectives, and trust that the universe is guiding you towards the right person at the right time. Focus on cultivating a deep sense of self-love and self-worth, and on attracting partners who reflect your highest values and desires.

Career:

In your career, June 2025 is a month of innovation, collaboration, and personal growth. With Mars, the planet of action and energy, traveling through your 11th house of groups, friends, and community for most of the month, you may feel a strong desire to connect with like-minded individuals, join forces with others, and make a positive impact in the world.

This is a time to network, collaborate, and share your ideas and talents with others. You may be invited to join a new team, organization, or project that aligns with your values and goals. Be open to new opportunities and perspectives, and trust that the universe is guiding you towards your highest potential and purpose.

However, the Venus-Saturn square on June 12th may bring any underlying fears, doubts, or limitations around your career and public image to the surface. This is an opportunity to confront any self-sabotaging behaviors or patterns, and to cultivate a deeper sense of self-trust and self-confidence. Remember that your worth and value are not defined by external validation or success, but by your own inner sense of purpose and integrity.

Finances:

In finances, June 2025 is a month of abundance, prosperity, and personal growth. With Venus traveling through your sign for most of the month, you may experience a heightened sense of self-worth, value, and deserving. This is a time to trust in your own talents and abilities, and to attract financial opportunities and resources that align with your highest values and goals.

The New Moon in Gemini on June 25th will activate your 2nd house of money, resources, and self-worth, inviting you to set powerful intentions around abundance, prosperity, and financial freedom. This is a time to cultivate a mindset of gratitude, generosity, and positive expectation, and to trust that the universe is always providing for your needs and desires.

However, the Venus-Saturn square on June 12th may bring any underlying fears, doubts, or limitations around money and security to the surface. This is an opportunity to confront any scarcity mentality or limiting beliefs, and to cultivate a deeper sense of trust and faith in the abundance of the universe. Remember that your true wealth and security come from within, and that you are always supported and provided for by a loving and benevolent universe.

Health:

In health, June 2025 is a month of vitality, resilience, and personal growth. With Venus traveling through your sign for most of the month, you may feel a heightened sense of physical vitality, sensuality, and well-being. This is a time to prioritize your self-care and self-love, and to cultivate daily practices and habits that support your overall health and happiness.

Take time to rest, recharge, and listen to your body's needs and signals. Engage in activities that bring you joy, relaxation, and a sense of connection to your inner self, such as massage, yoga, or spending time in nature. Nourish your body with healthy, whole foods, and limit your exposure to toxins, stress, and negative influences.

However, the Venus-Saturn square on June 12th may bring any underlying fears, doubts, or limitations around your health and well-being to the surface. This is an opportunity to confront any self-sabotaging behaviors or patterns, and to cultivate a deeper sense of self-compassion and self-acceptance. Remember that your body is a sacred temple, and that you deserve to treat yourself with love, kindness, and respect.

Travel:

In travel, June 2025 may bring unexpected opportunities for adventure, exploration, and personal growth. With Mars traveling through your 11th house of groups, friends, and community for most of the month, you may feel a strong desire to connect with others, explore new places and cultures, and expand your horizons.

Consider taking a trip with friends or joining a group tour or retreat that aligns with your interests and passions. This is a time to step outside your comfort zone, challenge your assumptions and beliefs, and open yourself up to new ideas and possibilities.

However, the Venus-Saturn square on June 12th may bring any underlying fears, doubts, or limitations around travel and exploration to the surface. This is an opportunity to confront any limiting beliefs or patterns that may be holding you back from true freedom and adventure. Remember that growth and expansion often require stepping into the unknown, and that every challenge is an opportunity for learning and transformation.

Insights from the Stars:

The celestial energies of June 2025 remind you of the power of self-love, self-worth, and personal empowerment. With Venus traveling through your sign and the New Moon in Gemini activating your 2nd house of money, resources, and self-worth, you are being called to celebrate your unique qualities and talents and to trust in your own value and worth.

This is a time to let go of any limiting beliefs or patterns that may be holding you back from true abundance, joy, and fulfillment. You are a powerful creator and manifester, and your thoughts, beliefs, and actions have the power to shape your reality and attract your deepest desires and dreams.

Stay open to the unexpected, and trust that every challenge or setback is an opportunity for growth, learning, and transformation. Remember that you are a divine being of love and light, and that your soul's journey is unfolding in perfect timing and alignment with your highest good.

Best Days of the Month:

June 1st: Jupiter biquintile Pluto, bringing opportunities for deep transformation, healing, and personal growth. Trust in the wisdom of your soul, and be open to new possibilities and perspectives.

June 4th: Saturn sextile Uranus, bringing a harmonious blend of stability and change, tradition and innovation. This is a time to make positive changes in your life that align with your highest values and goals.

June 11th: The Full Moon in Sagittarius illuminates your 8th house of intimacy, shared resources, and personal transformation. Let go of any fears or limitations that may be holding you back from true connection and abundance.

June 21st: The Sun enters Cancer, marking the Summer Solstice and a powerful time of spiritual growth and emotional healing. Nurture yourself and your loved ones, and trust in the wisdom of your heart.

June 25th: The New Moon in Gemini activates your 2nd house of money, resources, and self-worth. Set powerful intentions around abundance, prosperity, and financial freedom, and trust in your own value and deserving.

July 2025

Overview Horoscope for the Month:

Taurus, July 2025 is a month of personal growth, spiritual awakening, and positive change for you. The astrological energies are dynamic and transformative, with a series of powerful planetary alignments and eclipses inviting you to step into your power, embrace your authentic self, and create a life that aligns with your deepest values and desires.

The month begins with Mars, the planet of action and energy, entering Leo on July 18th, activating your 4th house of home, family, and emotional foundations. This transit will bring a renewed sense of passion, creativity, and self-expression to your personal life, and may inspire you to make positive changes in your living space or family dynamics.

The Full Moon in Capricorn on July 10th will illuminate your 9th house of travel, higher education, and spiritual growth, inviting you to expand your horizons, seek new adventures, and connect with your higher purpose. This is a time to let go of any limiting beliefs or patterns that may be holding you back from true freedom and fulfillment, and to trust in the wisdom and guidance of the universe.

Love:

In love, July 2025 is a month of passion, romance, and emotional depth. With Venus, your ruling planet, traveling through Cancer for most of the month, you may feel a strong desire for intimacy, security, and emotional connection in your relationships. This is a time to nurture your loved ones, express your feelings openly and authentically, and create a safe and supportive space for love to flourish.

If you're in a committed relationship, the Full Moon in Capricorn on July 10th may bring a renewed sense of commitment, stability, and long-term vision to your partnership. This is a time to discuss your shared goals and dreams, and to make plans for the future that align with your deepest values and desires. Be willing to compromise and find a balance between your individual needs and the needs of the relationship.

If you're single, the Mars-Venus conjunction in Leo on July 21st may bring exciting opportunities for romance and passion. This is a time to express your unique qualities and talents, and to attract partners who appreciate and celebrate your authentic self. Focus on cultivating a deep sense of self-love and self-worth, and trust that the universe will bring you the right person at the right time.

Career:

In your career, July 2025 is a month of ambition, leadership, and positive change. With the Sun traveling through your 3rd house of communication, learning, and networking for most of the month, you may feel a strong desire to share your ideas, skills, and talents with others, and to make a positive impact in your community or industry.

This is a time to network, collaborate, and seek out new opportunities for growth and advancement. You may be invited to speak, write, or teach about your area of expertise, or to take on a leadership role in a project or organization that aligns with your values and goals.

However, the Full Moon in Capricorn on July 10th may bring any underlying fears, doubts, or limitations around your career and public image to the surface. This is an opportunity to confront any self-sabotaging behaviors or patterns, and to cultivate a deeper sense of self-trust and self-confidence. Remember that your worth and value are not defined by external validation or success, but by your own inner sense of purpose and integrity.

Finances:

In finances, July 2025 is a month of abundance, prosperity, and positive change. With Venus traveling through your 3rd house of communication and networking for most of the month, you may experience unexpected opportunities for financial growth and success through your connections and interactions with others.

This is a time to share your ideas, skills, and talents with the world, and to attract abundance and prosperity through your unique gifts and contributions. Trust in your own value and worth, and be open to receiving support, resources, and opportunities from unexpected sources.

However, the Full Moon in Capricorn on July 10th may bring any underlying fears, doubts, or limitations around money and security to the surface. This is an opportunity to confront any scarcity mentality or limiting beliefs, and to cultivate a deeper sense of trust and faith in the abundance of the universe. Remember that your true wealth and security come from within, and that you are always supported and provided for by a loving and benevolent universe.

Health:

In health, July 2025 is a month of vitality, resilience, and emotional healing. With Mars entering Leo on July 18th, activating your 4th house of home, family, and emotional foundations, you may feel a renewed sense of energy, passion, and creativity in your personal life. This is a time to prioritize your self-care and self-expression, and to cultivate daily practices and habits that support your physical, emotional, and spiritual well-being.

Take time to rest, recharge, and listen to your body's needs and signals. Engage in activities that bring you joy, relaxation, and a sense of connection to your inner child, such as dancing, singing, or playing. Nourish your body with healthy, whole foods, and limit your exposure to toxins, stress, and negative influences.

However, the Full Moon in Capricorn on July 10th may bring any underlying fears, doubts, or limitations around your health and well-being to the surface. This is an opportunity to confront any self-sabotaging behaviors or patterns, and to cultivate a deeper sense of self-compassion and self-acceptance. Remember that your body is a sacred temple, and that you deserve to treat yourself with love, kindness, and respect.

Travel:

In travel, July 2025 may bring exciting opportunities for adventure, exploration, and personal growth. With the Full Moon in Capricorn on July 10th illuminating your 9th house of travel, higher education, and spiritual growth, you may feel a strong desire to expand your horizons, seek new experiences, and connect with your higher purpose.

Consider taking a trip or enrolling in a course or workshop that aligns with your interests and passions. This is a time to step outside your comfort zone, challenge your assumptions and beliefs, and open yourself up to new ideas and possibilities.

However, the Full Moon in Capricorn may also bring any underlying fears, doubts, or limitations around travel and exploration to the surface. This is an opportunity to confront any limiting beliefs or patterns that may be holding you back from true freedom and adventure. Remember that growth and expansion often require stepping into the unknown, and that every challenge is an opportunity for learning and transformation.

Insights from the Stars:

The celestial energies of July 2025 remind you of the power of self-expression, creativity, and emotional healing. With Mars entering Leo, activating your 4th house of home, family, and emotional foundations, and Venus traveling through Cancer, your 3rd house of communication and connection, you are being called to express your authentic self, nurture your loved ones, and create a life that aligns with your deepest values and desires.

This is a time to let go of any masks, facades, or limitations that may be holding you back from true joy, fulfillment, and self-realization. You are a powerful creator and manifester, and your thoughts, beliefs, and actions have the power to shape your reality and attract your deepest desires and dreams.

Stay open to the unexpected, and trust that every challenge or setback is an opportunity for growth, learning, and transformation. Remember that you are a divine being of love and light, and that your soul's journey is unfolding in perfect timing and alignment with your highest good.

Best Days of the Month:

July 1st: The Sun conjunct Mercury, bringing clarity, insight, and positive communication to your interactions and relationships. This is a great time to share your ideas, express your feelings, and connect with others.

July 10th: The Full Moon in Capricorn illuminates your 9th house of travel, higher education, and spiritual growth. Let go of any limiting beliefs or patterns that may be holding you back from true freedom and fulfillment, and trust in the wisdom and guidance of the universe.

July 18th: Mars enters Leo, activating your 4th house of home, family, and emotional foundations. This is a time to express your passion, creativity, and self-expression in your personal life, and to make positive changes in your living space or family dynamics.

July 22nd: The Sun enters Leo, marking the beginning of a new cycle of creativity, self-expression, and personal growth. Celebrate your unique qualities and talents, and trust in your own inner light and power.

July 30th: The New Moon in Leo invites you to set powerful intentions around your personal goals, desires, and self-expression. Trust in your own worth and value, and take bold steps towards creating a life that aligns with your authentic self and purpose.

August 2025

Overview Horoscope for the Month:

Taurus, August 2025 is a month of self-discovery, spiritual growth, and personal empowerment for you. The astrological energies are intense and transformative, with a series of powerful planetary alignments and eclipses inviting you to dive deep into your inner world, confront your shadows, and emerge with a renewed sense of purpose and passion.

The month begins with Venus, your ruling planet, entering Leo on August 25th, activating your 4th house of home, family, and emotional foundations. This transit will bring a heightened sense of creativity, self-expression, and joy to your personal life, and may inspire you to make positive changes in your living space or family dynamics.

The Full Moon in Aquarius on August 9th will illuminate your 10th house of career, public image, and long-term goals, inviting you to reassess your professional path, let go of any limiting beliefs or patterns, and align your work with your authentic self and purpose. This is a time to trust in your unique talents and abilities, and to make bold moves towards your dreams and aspirations.

Love:

In love, August 2025 is a month of emotional depth, vulnerability, and transformation. With Venus traveling through Cancer for most of the month, you may feel a strong desire for intimacy, security, and emotional connection in your relationships. This is a time to nurture your loved ones, express your feelings openly and authentically, and create a safe and supportive space for love to flourish.

If you're in a committed relationship, the Full Moon in Aquarius on August 9th may bring unexpected insights or revelations about your partnership. This is an opportunity to have honest, open conversations with your partner about your needs, desires, and long-term goals, and to make any necessary changes or adjustments to your relationship dynamics. Be willing to let go of any expectations or attachments that may be holding you back from true intimacy and growth.

If you're single, the Venus-Pluto opposition on August 26th may bring intense feelings of desire, passion, and transformation to your love life. This is a time to confront any fears or shadows around intimacy and vulnerability, and to attract partners who reflect your deepest values and desires. Focus on cultivating a deep sense of self-love and self-worth, and trust that the universe will bring you the right person at the right time.

Career:

In your career, August 2025 is a month of innovation, leadership, and positive change. With the Full Moon in Aquarius on August 9th illuminating your 10th house of career, public image, and long-term goals, you may feel a strong desire to make a meaningful impact in your work, and to align your professional path with your authentic self and purpose.

This is a time to reassess your career goals, let go of any limiting beliefs or patterns, and take bold steps towards your dreams and aspirations. You may be recognized for your unique talents and contributions, or offered new opportunities for growth and advancement. Trust in your own worth and value, and don't be afraid to take risks or think outside the box.

However, the Venus-Pluto opposition on August 26th may bring any underlying fears, doubts, or power struggles in your career to the surface. This is an opportunity to confront any self-sabotaging behaviors or patterns, and to cultivate a deeper sense of self-trust and self-confidence. Remember that your worth and value are not defined by external validation or success, but by your own inner sense of purpose and integrity.

Finances:

In finances, August 2025 is a month of abundance, prosperity, and positive change. With Venus traveling through your 4th house of home and family for most of the month, you may experience unexpected opportunities for financial growth and success through your personal connections and relationships.

This is a time to trust in the abundance and support of the universe, and to attract wealth and resources through your unique gifts and contributions. Focus on cultivating a mindset of gratitude, generosity, and positive expectation, and be open to receiving blessings and opportunities from unexpected sources.

However, the Full Moon in Aquarius on August 9th may bring any underlying fears, doubts, or limitations around money and security to the surface. This is an opportunity to confront any scarcity mentality or limiting beliefs, and to cultivate a deeper sense of trust and faith in the abundance of the universe. Remember that your true wealth and security come from within, and that you are always supported and provided for by a loving and benevolent universe.

Health:

In health, August 2025 is a month of vitality, resilience, and emotional healing. With Mars traveling through Virgo for most of the month, activating your 5th house of creativity, self-expression, and joy, you may feel a renewed sense of energy, passion, and enthusiasm for life. This is a time to prioritize your self-care and self-love, and to cultivate daily practices and habits that support your physical, emotional, and spiritual well-being.

Take time to rest, recharge, and listen to your body's needs and signals. Engage in activities that bring you pleasure, relaxation, and a sense of connection to your inner child, such as art, music, or play. Nourish your body with healthy, whole foods, and limit your exposure to toxins, stress, and negative influences.

However, the Full Moon in Aquarius on August 9th may bring any underlying fears, doubts, or limitations around your health and well-being to the surface. This is an opportunity to confront any self-sabotaging behaviors or patterns, and to cultivate a deeper sense of self-compassion and self-acceptance. Remember that your body is a sacred temple, and that you deserve to treat yourself with love, kindness, and respect.

Travel:

In travel, August 2025 may bring opportunities for personal growth, self-discovery, and spiritual awakening. With the Sun traveling through your 5th house of creativity, self-expression, and joy for most of the month, you may feel a strong desire to explore new places, try new things, and connect with your inner child.

Consider taking a trip or enrolling in a workshop or retreat that aligns with your interests and passions. This is a time to step outside your comfort zone, challenge your assumptions and beliefs, and open yourself up to new ideas and possibilities.

However, the Full Moon in Aquarius on August 9th may bring any underlying fears, doubts, or limitations around travel and exploration to the surface. This is an opportunity to confront any limiting beliefs or patterns that may be holding you back from true freedom and adventure. Remember that growth and expansion often require stepping into the unknown, and that every challenge is an opportunity for learning and transformation.

Insights from the Stars:

The celestial energies of August 2025 remind you of the power of self-love, self-expression, and personal transformation. With Venus traveling through your 4th house of home and family, and Mars activating your 5th house of creativity and joy, you are being called to connect with your inner child, express your authentic self, and create a life that aligns with your deepest values and desires.

This is a time to let go of any masks, facades, or limitations that may be holding you back from true happiness, fulfillment, and self-realization. You are a powerful creator and manifester, and your thoughts, beliefs, and actions have the power to shape your reality and attract your deepest desires and dreams.

Stay open to the unexpected, and trust that every challenge or setback is an opportunity for growth, learning, and transformation. Remember that you are a divine being of love and light, and that your soul's journey is unfolding in perfect timing and alignment with your highest good.

Best Days of the Month:

August 3rd: Uranus quintile True Node, bringing unexpected insights, breakthroughs, and opportunities for growth and change. Trust your intuition and be open to new possibilities and perspectives.

August 11th: Mercury goes direct in Leo, bringing clarity, insight, and forward momentum to your communication, ideas, and plans. Express yourself with confidence and authenticity, and trust in the power of your voice and vision.

August 16th: The Last Quarter Moon in Taurus illuminates your 1st house of self and identity, inviting you to let go of any limiting beliefs or patterns that may be holding you back from true self-expression and personal growth. Embrace your unique qualities and talents, and trust in your own worth and value.

August 23rd: The New Moon in Virgo activates your 5th house of creativity, self-expression, and joy, inviting you to set powerful intentions around your personal goals, desires, and passions. Trust in the power of play, pleasure, and self-love, and take bold steps towards creating a life that brings you joy and fulfillment.

August 28th: Uranus sextile Neptune, bringing a harmonious blend of innovation and inspiration, practicality and spirituality. This is a great time to connect with your higher purpose, trust in the wisdom of the universe, and make positive changes in your life that align with your deepest values and dreams.

September 2025

Overview Horoscope for the Month:

Taurus, September 2025 is a month of introspection, spiritual growth, and personal transformation for you. The astrological energies are intense and profound, with a series of powerful planetary alignments and eclipses inviting you to go within, connect with your inner wisdom, and align your life with your deepest values and purpose.

The month begins with Saturn, the planet of structure, responsibility, and karmic lessons, entering Pisces on September 1st, activating your 11th house of friends, groups, and social causes. This transit, which will last until 2028, will bring a heightened sense of duty, commitment, and purpose to your social life and community involvement, and may challenge you to let go of any superficial connections or activities that no longer serve your highest good.

The Full Moon Total Lunar Eclipse in Pisces on September 7th will illuminate your 11th house, bringing powerful insights, revelations, and shifts in your friendships, networks, and long-term goals. This is a time to trust in the wisdom of the universe, surrender to the flow of life, and allow any necessary endings or beginnings to unfold in divine timing.

Love:

In love, September 2025 is a month of emotional depth, spiritual connection, and karmic healing. With Venus, your ruling planet, traveling through Virgo for most of the month, you may feel a strong desire for authenticity, purity, and service in your relationships. This is a time to focus on the practical details of love, and to cultivate a sense of devotion, humility, and unconditional acceptance towards yourself and others.

If you're in a committed relationship, the Saturn-Neptune conjunction on September 8th may bring a powerful opportunity for spiritual growth, emotional healing, and karmic resolution in your partnership. This is a time to let go of any illusions, expectations, or attachments that may be holding you back from true intimacy and connection, and to trust in the divine plan for your relationship. Be willing to do the inner work of forgiveness, compassion, and unconditional love, and to support each other's soul growth and evolution.

If you're single, the New Moon Partial Solar Eclipse in Virgo on September 21st may bring unexpected opportunities for love and romance through your work, health, or service to others. This is a time to focus on cultivating a deep sense of self-love, self-care, and self-respect, and to attract partners who reflect your highest values and aspirations. Trust in the wisdom of your heart, and be open to the magic and synchronicity of the universe.

Career:

In your career, September 2025 is a month of purpose, service, and spiritual alignment. With Mars, the planet of action and drive, entering Scorpio on September 22nd, activating your 7th house of partnerships and collaboration, you may feel a strong desire to join forces with others, create powerful alliances, and make a meaningful impact in your work and community.

This is a time to focus on the deeper purpose and meaning of your career, and to align your professional path with your soul's mission and values. You may be called to take on a leadership role, mentor others, or use your skills and talents to serve a higher cause. Trust in your unique gifts and contributions, and don't be afraid to take bold steps towards your dreams and aspirations.

However, the Full Moon Total Lunar Eclipse in Pisces on September 7th may bring any underlying fears, doubts, or limitations in your career to the surface. This is an opportunity to confront any self-sabotaging behaviors or patterns, and to cultivate a deeper sense of trust, faith, and surrender in your professional journey. Remember that your true success and fulfillment come from living in alignment with your soul's purpose, and that every challenge is an opportunity for growth and transformation.

Finances:

In finances, September 2025 is a month of abundance, prosperity, and spiritual alignment. With Venus traveling through your 6th house of work, health, and service for most of the month, you may experience unexpected opportunities for financial growth and success through your practical skills, dedication, and commitment to excellence.

This is a time to focus on the deeper meaning and purpose of money, and to align your financial goals with your spiritual values and aspirations. Trust in the abundance and support of the universe, and be open to receiving blessings and opportunities from unexpected sources. Focus on cultivating a mindset of gratitude, generosity, and positive expectation, and be willing to share your resources and talents with others in need.

However, the Full Moon Total Lunar Eclipse in Pisces on September 7th may bring any underlying fears, doubts, or limitations around money and security to the surface. This is an opportunity to confront any scarcity mentality or limiting beliefs, and to cultivate a deeper sense of trust and faith in the divine plan for your life. Remember that your true wealth and security come from within, and that you are always supported and provided for by a loving and benevolent universe.

Health:

In health, September 2025 is a month of balance, purification, and spiritual alignment. With the Sun traveling through Virgo for most of the month, activating your 5th house of joy, creativity, and self-expression, you may feel a strong desire to prioritize your physical, emotional, and spiritual well-being, and to cultivate daily practices and habits that support your vitality, resilience, and inner peace.

This is a time to focus on the mind-body-spirit
connection, and to align your health and wellness goals
with your deepest values and aspirations. Take time to
rest, recharge, and listen to your body's wisdom and
guidance. Engage in activities that bring you joy,
pleasure, and a sense of connection to your inner child,
such as dance, art, or nature. Nourish your body with
clean, wholesome foods, and limit your exposure to
toxins, stress, and negative influences.

However, the Full Moon Total Lunar Eclipse in
Pisces on September 7th may bring any underlying
fears, doubts, or limitations around your health and
well-being to the surface. This is an opportunity to
confront any self-sabotaging behaviors or patterns, and
to cultivate a deeper sense of self-compassion, self-
acceptance, and self-love. Remember that your body is
a sacred temple, and that you deserve to treat yourself
with kindness, respect, and reverence.

Travel:

In travel, September 2025 may bring opportunities
for spiritual growth, personal transformation, and
karmic healing. With Saturn entering Pisces on
September 1st, activating your 11th house of friends,
groups, and social causes, you may feel a strong desire

to travel with like-minded individuals, join a spiritual community or retreat, or engage in a humanitarian mission or service project.

This is a time to focus on the deeper meaning and purpose of your travels, and to align your adventures with your soul's journey and evolution. Consider taking a pilgrimage to a sacred site, attending a transformational workshop or conference, or immersing yourself in a foreign culture or way of life that expands your perspective and challenges your assumptions.

However, the Full Moon Total Lunar Eclipse in Pisces on September 7th may bring any underlying fears, doubts, or limitations around travel and exploration to the surface. This is an opportunity to confront any limiting beliefs or patterns that may be holding you back from true freedom and adventure, and to cultivate a deeper sense of trust, faith, and surrender in the journey of life. Remember that every experience, whether pleasant or challenging, is an opportunity for growth, learning, and transformation.

Insights from the Stars:

The celestial energies of September 2025 remind you of the power of surrender, faith, and spiritual alignment. With Saturn entering Pisces, activating your 11th house of friends, groups, and social causes, and the Full Moon Total Lunar Eclipse illuminating this same area of your chart, you are being called to let go of any superficial connections or activities that no longer serve your highest good, and to align your social life and community involvement with your soul's purpose and values.

This is a time to trust in the wisdom and guidance of the universe, and to allow any necessary endings or beginnings to unfold in divine timing. You are a powerful co-creator and manifestor, and your thoughts, beliefs, and actions have the power to shape your reality and attract your deepest desires and dreams. Stay open to the magic and synchronicity of life, and trust that every challenge or setback is an opportunity for growth, healing, and transformation.

Remember that you are a divine being of love and light, and that your soul's journey is unfolding in perfect harmony with the greater plan of the universe. Embrace your unique gifts and talents, and trust in your ability to make a positive difference in the world, one person and one moment at a time.

Best Days of the Month:

September 3rd: Jupiter trine True Node, bringing opportunities for spiritual growth, karmic healing, and alignment with your soul's purpose. Trust in the wisdom and guidance of the universe, and be open to new possibilities and perspectives.

September 7th: The Full Moon Total Lunar Eclipse in Pisces illuminates your 11th house of friends, groups, and social causes, bringing powerful insights, revelations, and shifts in your social life and community involvement. Let go of any superficial connections or activities that no longer serve your highest good, and trust in the divine plan for your life.

September 18th: Mercury enters Libra, activating your 6th house of work, health, and service. This is a great time to focus on the practical details of your life, communicate your needs and boundaries clearly, and cultivate a sense of balance, harmony, and cooperation in your daily routines and relationships.

September 21st: The New Moon Partial Solar Eclipse in Virgo activates your 5th house of joy, creativity, and self-expression, inviting you to set powerful intentions around your personal goals, desires, and passions. Trust in the power of play, pleasure, and self-love, and take bold steps towards creating a life that brings you happiness and fulfillment.

September 29th: Venus enters Libra, bringing a harmonious and balanced energy to your work, health, and service sector. Focus on creating beauty, peace, and harmony in your daily life, and cultivate a sense of gratitude, grace, and diplomacy in your interactions with others.

October 2025

Overview Horoscope for the Month:

Taurus, October 2025 is a month of new
beginnings, personal growth, and spiritual awakening
for you. The astrological energies are intense and
transformative, with a series of powerful planetary
alignments and eclipses inviting you to embrace
change, let go of the past, and step into your highest
potential and purpose.

The month begins with Venus, your ruling planet,
entering Scorpio on October 6th, activating your 7th
house of partnerships, relationships, and self-
awareness. This transit will bring a heightened sense of
intensity, depth, and passion to your connections with
others, and may challenge you to confront any fears,
shadows, or power dynamics that may be holding you
back from true intimacy and authenticity.

The New Moon Partial Solar Eclipse in Libra on
October 21st will illuminate your 6th house of work,
health, and service, bringing powerful opportunities for

new beginnings, fresh starts, and positive changes in your daily routines, habits, and lifestyle. This is a time to set clear intentions, take inspired action, and trust in the unfolding of your path and purpose.

Love:

In love, October 2025 is a month of intensity, transformation, and spiritual growth. With Venus traveling through Scorpio for most of the month, you may feel a strong desire for deep connection, emotional honesty, and soul-level intimacy in your relationships. This is a time to dive beneath the surface, explore your desires and fears, and cultivate a sense of trust, vulnerability, and empowerment in your interactions with others.

If you're in a committed relationship, the Venus-Uranus opposition on October 11th may bring unexpected insights, revelations, or shifts in your partnership. This is an opportunity to break free from any limiting patterns or dynamics, and to embrace a new level of freedom, individuality, and authenticity in your connection. Be willing to have honest conversations, take risks, and explore new ways of relating that honor both your needs and your partner's.

If you're single, the New Moon Partial Solar Eclipse in Libra on October 21st may bring powerful opportunities for new love, romance, and self-discovery. This is a time to focus on cultivating a deep sense of self-love, self-respect, and self-awareness, and to attract partners who reflect your highest values and aspirations. Trust in the wisdom of your heart, and be open to the magic and synchronicity of the universe.

Career:

In your career, October 2025 is a month of innovation, collaboration, and positive change. With Mercury, the planet of communication and learning, entering Scorpio on October 6th, activating your 7th house of partnerships and cooperation, you may feel a strong desire to join forces with others, share your ideas and insights, and create powerful alliances and networks in your professional life.

This is a time to focus on the deeper purpose and meaning of your work, and to align your career path with your soul's mission and values. You may be called to take on a leadership role, mentor others, or use your skills and talents to make a positive impact in your industry or community. Trust in your unique gifts and contributions, and don't be afraid to take bold steps towards your dreams and aspirations.

However, the Full Moon in Aries on October 6th may bring any underlying fears, doubts, or limitations in your career to the surface. This is an opportunity to confront any self-sabotaging behaviors or patterns, and to cultivate a deeper sense of courage, confidence, and self-belief in your professional journey. Remember that your true success and fulfillment come from living in alignment with your soul's purpose, and that every challenge is an opportunity for growth and transformation.

Finances:

In finances, October 2025 is a month of abundance, prosperity, and spiritual alignment. With Jupiter, the planet of expansion and abundance, traveling through your 3rd house of communication, learning, and self-expression for most of the month, you may experience unexpected opportunities for financial growth and success through your ideas, insights, and creative talents.

This is a time to focus on the power of your thoughts, words, and beliefs, and to align your financial goals with your spiritual values and aspirations. Trust in the abundance and support of the universe, and be open to receiving blessings and opportunities from unexpected sources. Focus on cultivating a mindset of gratitude, generosity, and positive expectation, and be willing to share your resources and talents with others in need.

However, the Full Moon in Aries on October 6th may bring any underlying fears, doubts, or limitations around money and security to the surface. This is an opportunity to confront any scarcity mentality or limiting beliefs, and to cultivate a deeper sense of trust and faith in the divine plan for your life. Remember that your true wealth and security come from within, and that you are always supported and provided for by a loving and benevolent universe.

Health:

In health, October 2025 is a month of transformation, healing, and spiritual growth. With Pluto, the planet of power and regeneration, turning direct in your 9th house of higher wisdom, beliefs, and personal growth on October 13th, you may feel a strong desire to deepen your understanding of yourself, your purpose, and your place in the world, and to release any limiting patterns or behaviors that may be holding you back from optimal health and well-being.

This is a time to focus on the mind-body-spirit connection, and to align your health and wellness goals with your deepest values and aspirations. Take time to rest, recharge, and listen to your body's wisdom and guidance. Engage in activities that bring you a sense of peace, clarity, and inner strength, such as meditation, yoga, or energy healing. Nourish your body with clean, wholesome foods, and limit your exposure to toxins, stress, and negative influences.

However, the New Moon Partial Solar Eclipse in Libra on October 21st may bring powerful opportunities for new beginnings and positive changes in your daily routines, habits, and lifestyle. This is a time to set clear intentions, take inspired action, and trust in the unfolding of your path and purpose. Remember that your health and well-being are a reflection of your inner state of being, and that true healing comes from aligning your mind, body, and spirit with the wisdom and guidance of the universe.

Travel:

In travel, October 2025 may bring opportunities for personal growth, self-discovery, and spiritual awakening. With Mars, the planet of action and adventure, entering Sagittarius on October 29th, activating your 8th house of transformation, intimacy, and shared resources, you may feel a strong desire to explore new horizons, challenge your comfort zone, and deepen your understanding of yourself and others.

This is a time to focus on the deeper meaning and purpose of your travels, and to align your adventures with your soul's journey and evolution. Consider taking a trip that allows you to connect with your inner wisdom, explore your shadows and fears, and cultivate a sense of trust, surrender, and empowerment. This could be a solo journey, a couple's retreat, or a group adventure that challenges you to grow and transform in powerful ways.

However, the Full Moon in Aries on October 6th may bring any underlying fears, doubts, or limitations around travel and exploration to the surface. This is an opportunity to confront any limiting beliefs or patterns that may be holding you back from true freedom and adventure, and to cultivate a deeper sense of courage, confidence, and self-belief in the journey of life.

Remember that every experience, whether pleasant or challenging, is an opportunity for growth, learning, and transformation.

Insights from the Stars:

The celestial energies of October 2025 remind you of the power of transformation, authenticity, and spiritual growth. With Venus entering Scorpio, activating your 7th house of partnerships and self-awareness, and the New Moon Partial Solar Eclipse illuminating your 6th house of work, health, and service, you are being called to embrace change, let go of the past, and step into your highest potential and purpose.

This is a time to trust in the wisdom and guidance of the universe, and to allow any necessary endings or beginnings to unfold in divine timing. You are a powerful co-creator and manifestor, and your thoughts, beliefs, and actions have the power to shape your reality and attract your deepest desires and dreams. Stay open to the magic and synchronicity of life, and trust that every challenge or setback is an opportunity for growth, healing, and transformation.

Remember that you are a divine being of love and light, and that your soul's journey is unfolding in perfect harmony with the greater plan of the universe. Embrace your unique gifts and talents, and trust in your ability to make a positive difference in the world, one person and one moment at a time.

Best Days of the Month:

October 7th: Mars enters Scorpio, activating your 7th house of partnerships and self-awareness. This is a great time to focus on deepening your connections with others, exploring your desires and fears, and cultivating a sense of trust, vulnerability, and empowerment in your relationships.

October 13th: Pluto turns direct in your 9th house of higher wisdom, beliefs, and personal growth. This is a powerful time for spiritual awakening, inner transformation, and the release of any limiting patterns or behaviors that may be holding you back from your highest potential and purpose.

October 16th: The Last Quarter Moon in Cancer illuminates your 3rd house of communication, learning, and self-expression, inviting you to share your ideas and insights with others, explore new ways of thinking and being, and cultivate a sense of emotional intelligence and empathy in your interactions.

October 21st: The New Moon Partial Solar Eclipse in Libra activates your 6th house of work, health, and service, bringing powerful opportunities for new beginnings, fresh starts, and positive changes in your daily routines, habits, and lifestyle. Set clear intentions, take inspired action, and trust in the unfolding of your path and purpose.

October 29th: Mars enters Sagittarius, activating your 8th house of transformation, intimacy, and shared resources. This is a great time to explore new horizons, challenge your comfort zone, and deepen your understanding of yourself and others through travel, adventure, and personal growth.

November 2025

Overview Horoscope for the Month:

Welcome to November 2025, Taurus! This month promises to be a time of profound transformation, inner growth, and new beginnings. The astrological energies align to support your journey of self-discovery, urging you to embrace change, let go of old patterns, and trust in the unfolding of your unique path. With a powerful stellium of planets in Scorpio activating your 7th house of partnerships and relationships, you are called to dive deep into the realm of intimacy, vulnerability, and emotional authenticity.

November 2025 is a pivotal month for you, Taurus, as it marks a significant turning point in your personal and relational growth. The Sun, Mercury, and Venus all travel through the intense and transformative sign of Scorpio, illuminating your 7th house of one-on-one partnerships, marriage, and interpersonal dynamics. This cosmic alignment invites you to confront the shadows, fears, and power struggles that may be holding you back from true intimacy and

connection, and to embrace the healing power of
vulnerability, trust, and emotional honesty.

The New Moon in Scorpio on November 20th
brings a potent opportunity for new beginnings, fresh
starts, and deepening commitments in your closest
relationships. Set intentions for the kind of partnerships
you wish to attract or nurture, focusing on the qualities
of authenticity, depth, and soul-level connection.

Love:

In matters of the heart, November 2025 emphasizes
the importance of emotional intensity, psychological
depth, and transformative intimacy. With Venus, your
ruling planet, in the mysterious and magnetic sign of
Scorpio until the 30th, you may find yourself craving a
soul-level bond with your partner, one that goes
beyond surface-level attraction and into the realm of
deep, raw, and vulnerable connection. This is a time to
confront any fears, secrets, or power dynamics that
may be blocking the flow of love and trust in your
relationships, and to cultivate a space of safety,
honesty, and emotional authenticity.

For single Taureans, the New Moon in Scorpio on
November 20th brings a powerful opportunity to set

intentions for the kind of partner and relationship you truly desire. Focus on the qualities of depth, intensity, and emotional connection, and trust that the universe will guide you towards individuals who resonate with your soul's yearnings. Be open to unexpected encounters and connections, as they may hold the key to profound growth and transformation.

For Taureans in committed relationships, this month invites you to take your connection to a deeper, more intimate level. The Full Moon in Taurus on November 5th illuminates your 1st house of self, identity, and personal desires, urging you to assert your needs, boundaries, and authentic self-expression within the context of your partnership. Have honest, vulnerable conversations with your partner about your fears, desires, and dreams, and work together to create a dynamic of mutual support, empowerment, and growth.

Career:

Your career sector is activated this month, Taurus, with Mars, the planet of action and ambition, traveling through the expansive and visionary sign of Sagittarius. This cosmic placement ignites your 8th house of shared resources, investments, and transformative power, urging you to take bold steps towards your long-term goals and aspirations. Trust your instincts and intuition when it comes to making strategic moves or taking calculated risks in your professional life, as they may lead to significant breakthroughs and opportunities for growth.

The New Moon in Scorpio on November 20th may bring unexpected shifts or changes in your work partnerships or collaborations. Embrace the transformative power of letting go of what no longer serves your highest good, and trust that any endings or new beginnings are ultimately guiding you towards your true path and purpose.

Finances:

November 2025 brings a focus on joint finances, shared resources, and the psychological dynamics of money and power. With the Sun, Mercury, and Venus activating your 8th house of investments, debts, and other people's resources, you are called to confront any fears, shadows, or limiting beliefs around financial intimacy and interdependence. This is a time to have honest, transparent conversations with your partner or trusted advisors about your financial goals, needs, and strategies, and to cultivate a mindset of abundance, trust, and mutual support.

The Full Moon in Taurus on November 5th may bring a culmination or turning point in your personal financial situation, urging you to assert your values, needs, and desires when it comes to money and material security. Trust your instincts and practical wisdom when making financial decisions, and remember that true wealth and abundance come from a place of inner worth and self-sufficiency.

Health:

Your physical and emotional well-being are highlighted this month, Taurus, as the intense and transformative energies of Scorpio activate your 7th house of one-on-one relationships and interpersonal dynamics. This cosmic placement may bring up deep-seated emotions, fears, or patterns related to intimacy, vulnerability, and power dynamics, urging you to confront and heal any wounds or blocks that may be impacting your overall health and vitality.

Make time for self-care practices that support your emotional and psychological well-being, such as therapy, journaling, or deep conversations with trusted friends and loved ones. Focus on cultivating a sense of inner balance, resilience, and emotional authenticity, and trust that any challenges or discomforts that arise are ultimately guiding you towards greater wholeness and healing.

Travel:

November 2025 may bring opportunities for transformative travel experiences or journeys of self-discovery, Taurus. With Mars, the planet of action and adventure, in the expansive and philosophical sign of Sagittarius, you may feel called to explore new horizons, both literally and figuratively. Consider planning a trip or retreat that allows you to dive deep into your psyche, confront your fears and shadows, and emerge with a renewed sense of purpose and perspective.

If physical travel is not possible, consider embarking on an inner journey through practices such as meditation, dream work, or shamanic journeying. Trust that any insights, revelations, or breakthroughs that arise are ultimately guiding you towards greater self-awareness, growth, and transformation.

Insights from the Stars:

The celestial energies of November 2025 remind you of the power of vulnerability, authenticity, and emotional depth, Taurus. As you navigate the intense and transformative energies of Scorpio, trust that you are being called to confront your shadows, heal your wounds, and emerge with a renewed sense of strength, resilience, and self-awareness.

Remember that true intimacy and connection require a willingness to be seen, heard, and accepted in all of your raw, messy, and beautiful humanity. Embrace the power of vulnerability, trust, and emotional honesty, and know that you are worthy of love, respect, and belonging, just as you are.

Best Days of the Month:

November 5th: The Full Moon in your sign illuminates your 1st house of self, identity, and personal desires, urging you to assert your needs, boundaries, and authentic self-expression.

November 9th: Mercury stations retrograde in Scorpio, inviting you to reflect on your communication patterns, relationship dynamics, and emotional needs.

November 20th: The New Moon in Scorpio brings a powerful opportunity for new beginnings, fresh starts, and deepening commitments in your closest relationships.

November 23rd: Jupiter stations direct in Taurus, ending its retrograde phase and bringing renewed opportunities for growth, expansion, and abundance in your personal and professional life.

November 30th: Venus enters Sagittarius, igniting your 8th house of intimacy, shared resources, and transformative power, and bringing a sense of adventure, optimism, and growth to your relationships and financial dealings.

December 2025

Overview Horoscope for the Month:

Welcome to December 2025, Taurus! This month promises to be a time of inner reflection, spiritual growth, and profound transformation. As the year comes to a close, the astrological energies align to support your journey of self-discovery, urging you to connect with your deepest truths, release old patterns and beliefs, and embrace the power of new beginnings. With a strong emphasis on your 8th house of intimacy, shared resources, and personal transformation, you are called to dive deep into the realms of vulnerability, trust, and emotional authenticity.

December 2025 is a significant month for you, Taurus, as it marks the beginning of a powerful new cycle of growth and self-discovery. The Sun's transit through the philosophical and expansive sign of Sagittarius until the 21st illuminates your 8th house of deep emotional connections, psychological healing, and spiritual transformation. This cosmic placement invites you to confront your fears, shadows, and limiting beliefs, and to embrace the power of surrender, faith, and inner wisdom.

The New Moon in Sagittarius on December 19th brings a potent opportunity for setting intentions, planting seeds, and embarking on a new journey of personal and spiritual growth. Focus on the areas of your life where you wish to experience greater depth, meaning, and purpose, and trust that the universe will guide you towards the resources, support, and opportunities you need to thrive.

Love:

In matters of the heart, December 2025 emphasizes the importance of emotional intimacy, vulnerability, and spiritual connection. With Venus, your ruling planet, traveling through the intense and passionate sign of Scorpio until the 24th, you may find yourself craving a deep, soulful bond with your partner, one that goes beyond surface-level attraction and into the realm of raw, honest, and transformative love. This is a time to confront any fears, secrets, or power dynamics that may be blocking the flow of trust and intimacy in your relationships, and to cultivate a space of safety, acceptance, and emotional authenticity.

For single Taureans, the New Moon in Sagittarius on December 19th brings a powerful opportunity to set intentions for the kind of partner and relationship you truly desire. Focus on the qualities of depth, meaning, and spiritual connection, and trust that the universe will guide you towards individuals who resonate with your soul's yearnings. Be open to unexpected encounters and connections, as they may hold the key to profound growth and transformation.

For Taureans in committed relationships, this month invites you to take your connection to a deeper, more intimate level. The Full Moon in Gemini on December 4th illuminates your 2nd house of values, self-worth, and material resources, urging you to examine your beliefs and patterns around love, money, and security. Have honest, vulnerable conversations with your partner about your needs, desires, and fears, and work together to create a dynamic of mutual support, empowerment, and growth.

Career:

Your career sector is activated this month, Taurus, with Mars, the planet of action and ambition, entering the disciplined and pragmatic sign of Capricorn on the 15th. This cosmic placement ignites your 9th house of higher education, long-distance travel, and personal growth, urging you to expand your horizons, take on new challenges, and pursue your long-term goals with determination and focus. Trust your instincts and practical wisdom when it comes to making strategic moves or taking calculated risks in your professional life, as they may lead to significant breakthroughs and opportunities for advancement.

The New Moon in Sagittarius on December 19th may bring unexpected shifts or changes in your work environment or job responsibilities. Embrace the power of adaptability, flexibility, and positive thinking, and trust that any endings or new beginnings are ultimately guiding you towards your true path and purpose.

Finances:

December 2025 brings a focus on shared finances, investments, and the psychological dynamics of money and power. With Venus, your ruling planet, traveling through the intense and transformative sign of Scorpio until the 24th, you are called to confront any fears, shadows, or limiting beliefs around financial intimacy and interdependence. This is a time to have honest, transparent conversations with your partner or trusted advisors about your financial goals, needs, and strategies, and to cultivate a mindset of abundance, trust, and mutual support.

The Full Moon in Gemini on December 4th may bring a culmination or turning point in your personal financial situation, urging you to communicate your values, needs, and desires when it comes to money and material security. Trust your instincts and practical wisdom when making financial decisions, and remember that true wealth and abundance come from a place of inner worth and self-sufficiency.

Health:

Your physical and emotional well-being are highlighted this month, Taurus, as the intense and transformative energies of Scorpio and Sagittarius activate your 8th house of deep emotional healing and spiritual growth. This cosmic placement may bring up deep-seated emotions, fears, or patterns related to intimacy, vulnerability, and power dynamics, urging you to confront and heal any wounds or blocks that may be impacting your overall health and vitality.

Make time for self-care practices that support your emotional and psychological well-being, such as therapy, journaling, or deep conversations with trusted friends and loved ones. Focus on cultivating a sense of inner balance, resilience, and emotional authenticity, and trust that any challenges or discomforts that arise are ultimately guiding you towards greater wholeness and healing.

Travel:

December 2025 may bring opportunities for transformative travel experiences or journeys of self-discovery, Taurus. With Mars, the planet of action and adventure, entering the disciplined and pragmatic sign of Capricorn on the 15th, you may feel called to explore new horizons, both literally and figuratively. Consider planning a trip or retreat that allows you to expand your mind, challenge your assumptions, and connect with your higher purpose and spiritual path.

If physical travel is not possible, consider embarking on an inner journey through practices such as meditation, yoga, or philosophical study. Trust that any insights, revelations, or breakthroughs that arise are ultimately guiding you towards greater self-awareness, growth, and transformation.

Insights from the Stars:

The celestial energies of December 2025 remind you of the power of surrender, faith, and inner wisdom, Taurus. As you navigate the intense and transformative energies of Scorpio and Sagittarius, trust that you are being called to let go of control, embrace the unknown, and connect with your deepest truths and highest potential.

Remember that true growth and transformation often require a willingness to step outside of your comfort zone, confront your fears and shadows, and trust in the journey of your soul. Embrace the power of vulnerability, authenticity, and emotional depth, and know that you are supported and guided by the universe every step of the way.

Best Days of the Month:

December 4th: The Full Moon in Gemini illuminates your 2nd house of values, self-worth, and material resources, urging you to communicate your needs, desires, and boundaries in your personal and financial relationships.

December 12th: Mercury enters Capricorn, bringing a sense of focus, discipline, and practicality to your thoughts, communications, and long-term planning.

December 19th: The New Moon in Sagittarius brings a powerful opportunity for setting intentions, planting seeds, and embarking on a new journey of personal and spiritual growth.

December 24th: Venus enters Capricorn, igniting your 9th house of higher education, long-distance travel, and personal growth, and bringing a sense of commitment, responsibility, and long-term vision to your relationships and creative pursuits.

December 29th: Jupiter squares Chiron, inviting you to confront and heal any wounds or blocks related to your sense of self-worth, security, and belonging, and to embrace the power of self-acceptance, compassion, and inner wisdom.

Printed in Great Britain
by Amazon